Christmas Time

OH JOY

This Book Belongs to

Christmas

Book 9

Content and Artwork by
Gooseberry Patch Company

LEISURE ARTS

VICE PRESIDENT AND EDITOR-IN-CHIEF: Sandra Graham Case
EXECUTIVE PUBLICATIONS DIRECTOR: Cheryl Nodine Gunnells
DESIGNER RELATIONS DIRECTOR: Debra Nettles
SENIOR PUBLICATIONS DIRECTOR: Susan White Sullivan
CRAFT PUBLICATIONS DIRECTOR: Deb Moore
KNIT AND CROCHET DIRECTOR: Mary Sullivan Hutcheson
DESIGN DIRECTOR: Cyndi Hansen
SPECIAL PROJECTS DIRECTOR: Susan Frantz Wiles
SENIOR PREPRESS DIRECTOR: Mark Hawkins
RETAIL MARKETING AND PHOTOGRAPHY DIRECTOR: Amy Vaughn

EDITORIAL STAFF

TECHNICAL
SENIOR TECHNICAL WRITER: Christina Kirkendoll
TECHNICAL WRITERS: Laura Siar Holyfield and Jennifer S. Hutchings
TECHNICAL ASSOCIATES: Katie Galucki, Sarah J. Green and Lois J. Long

EDITORIAL
EDITORIAL WRITER: Susan McManus Johnson

FOODS
FOODS ASSISTANT EDITOR: Laura Siar Holyfield
CONTRIBUTING TEST KITCHEN STAFF: Rose Glass Klein

OXMOOR HOUSE

EDITOR-IN-CHIEF: Nancy Fitzpatrick Wyatt
EXECUTIVE EDITOR: Susan Carlisle Payne
FOODS EDITOR: Kelly Hooper Troiano
PHOTOGRAPHY DIRECTOR: Jim Bathie
SENIOR PHOTO STYLIST: Kay E. Clarke
TEST KITCHENS DIRECTOR: Elizabeth Tyler Austin
TEST KITCHENS ASSISTANT DIRECTOR: Julie Christopher
FOOD STYLIST: Kelley Self Wilton
TEST KITCHENS STAFF: Nicole Lee Faber, Kathleen Royal Phillips, Catherine Crowell Steele and Ashley T. Strickland
TEST KITCHENS INTERN: Jane Chambliss
CONTRIBUTING PHOTOGRAPHER: Wes Fraser
CONTRIBUTING PHOTO STYLISTS: Lydia DeGaris Pursell, Mindy Shapiro and Katie Stoddard

DESIGN

DESIGN CAPTAIN: Anne Pulliam Stocks
DESIGNERS: Tonya Bradford Bates, Kim Kern, Kelly Reider, Lori Wenger and Becky Werle

ART

ART PUBLICATIONS DIRECTOR: Rhonda Shelby
ART CATEGORY MANAGER: Lora Puls
LEAD GRAPHIC ARTIST: Jeanne Zaffarano
IMAGING TECHNICIANS: Brian Hall, Stephanie Johnson and Mark R. Potter
PHOTOGRAPHY MANAGER: Katherine Atchison
CONTRIBUTING PHOTO STYLIST: Christy Myers
PUBLISHING SYSTEMS ADMINISTRATOR: Becky Riddle
PUBLISHING SYSTEMS ASSISTANTS: Clint Hanson and John Rose

BUSINESS STAFF

VICE PRESIDENT AND CHIEF OPERATIONS OFFICER: Tom Siebenmorgen
CORPORATE PLANNING AND DEVELOPMENT DIRECTOR: Laticia Mull Dittrich
VICE PRESIDENT, SALES AND MARKETING: Pam Stebbins
NATIONAL ACCOUNTS DIRECTOR: Martha Adams
SALES AND SERVICES DIRECTOR: Margaret Reinold
VICE PRESIDENT, OPERATIONS: Jim Dittrich
COMPTROLLER, OPERATIONS: Rob Thieme
RETAIL CUSTOMER SERVICE MANAGER: Stan Raynor
PRINT PRODUCTION MANAGER: Fred F. Pruss

Library of Congress Catalog Number 99-71586
Hardcover ISBN 1-60140-231-7 Softcover ISBN 1-60140-634-7
10 9 8 7 6 5 4 3 2 1

Christmas

Book 9

A LEISURE ARTS PUBLICATION

Christmas

Gooseberry Patch

This book is dedicated to our family & friends...
you make every day feel like Christmas!

How Did Gooseberry Patch Get Started?

You may know the story of Gooseberry Patch...the tale of two country friends who decided one day over the backyard fence to try their hands at the mail order business. Started in Jo Ann's kitchen back in 1984, Vickie & Jo Ann's dream of a "Country Store in Your Mailbox" has grown and grown to a 96-page catalog with over 400 products, including cookie cutters, Santas, snowmen, gift baskets, angels and our very own line of cookbooks! What an adventure for two country friends!

Through our catalogs and books, Gooseberry Patch has met country friends from all over the world. While sharing letters and phone calls, we found that our friends love to cook, decorate, garden and craft. We've created Kate, Holly & Mary Elizabeth to represent these devoted friends who live and love the country lifestyle the way we do. They're just like you & me... they're our "Country Friends®!"

Your friends at Gooseberry Patch

Mary Elizabeth ★ Holly ★ Kate ★ Spot

Table of Contents

sweet memories

Yummy stacks of sugar cookies, cut into shapes and sparkling with sugar or frosted in festive hues... homemade cookies conjure up the sweetest memories of the season. What better way to get together with friends than by hosting a party that centers around these and other traditional treats? Invite your family & friends over for a memorable Christmas of cookie decorating and ornament making! Instructions for the colorful invitation shown here are located on page 12.

*You're invited

PARTY TIME

at
Ron and Becky's
on
Mon, Dec. 18th
at
7:00 pm

Please join us for a fun-filled evening
of making cookies, ornaments,
Graham cracker houses, and
Memories.

Candy Tins

- spray adhesive
- assorted scrapbook papers
- small tins with lids
- alphabet stickers
- Christmas-motif transparencies
- thin glue dots
- assorted ribbons

Easy to make, these delightful tins make great gifts for family & friends. Working in a well-ventilated area, use spray adhesive to glue a paper piece to the top of each lid. Add a name with stickers. Wrap strips cut from the transparencies around the sides of the tin and secure with glue dots. Fill the tin with candy and tie with ribbon.

Decorative Charger

(also shown on pages 9, 12 and 14)

Serving sweets in style couldn't get any easier than this. Glue a scrapbook paper circle to the center of a charger and add a rickrack border along the rim. Place cookies or candy on a clear plate on top of the charger.

Ribbon "Candy"

Fold a length of ribbon back & forth to resemble old-fashioned Christmas candy. Attaching a bead at each end, sew thread through the center of the folded ribbon to hold in place. Fill a trifle bowl with these bright treats or add hangers and use them as tree ornaments.

Glass Candy (shown on the plate above) tastes as spectacular as it looks! The recipe for this colorful treat is on page 110.

I always entertain GREAT HOPES. ROBT. FROST

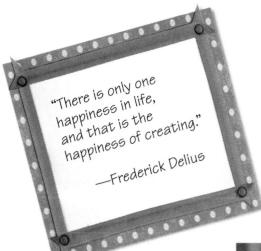

"There is only one happiness in life, and that is the happiness of creating."

—Frederick Delius

Invitations
(shown on page 8)
- rub-on letters
- white vellum
- vellum tape
- craft glue
- cardstock and scrapbook papers
- ribbons
- eyelets
- Christmas-motif transparencies
- brads
- circle punches
- adhesive foam dots

For each invitation, use a computer and rub-ons to print party information onto vellum and cut it into a tag. Layer and adhere the vellum tag on cardstock and paper tags. Knot ribbons through an eyelet at the top of the invitation. Make and decorate a paper pocket for each tag.

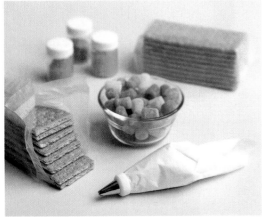

Royal Icing
5 c. powdered sugar
7 T. warm water
3 T. plus 1 t. meringue powder
1/2 t. lemon extract

Beat powdered sugar, water, meringue powder and lemon extract in a medium bowl with an electric mixer 7 to 10 minutes or until stiff. Makes 3 1/4 cups.

Graham Cracker Houses

- serrated knife
- whole graham cracker sheets
- Royal Icing
- plastic zipping bags or decorating bags with tips
- trays, plates or stands for the bases
- small hexagonal graham crackers
- assorted candies

No two alike…let each guest build a home-sweet-home! Once the houses are finished, put them on display under glass domes. Keep your papercrafting supplies handy and make tags to tie onto the domes.

1. For the front and back of each house, cut a roof peak at one short end of two cracker sheets.
2. Spoon icing into a bag and cut away one corner if using a zipping bag.
3. Squeezing icing onto the base for "cement" and icing the pieces together at the corners, stand the house front, sides (one whole sheet each) and back in the icing.
4. Ice the top edges of the house and lay two cracker sheets on top for the roof. For shingles, squeeze rows of icing onto the roof and add hexagonal crackers.
5. Add icing and candies to the house as you like.

Sugar Cookie Frosting
5 c. powdered sugar
5½ to 6½ T. water
1½ t. almond extract
paste food coloring

Combine powdered sugar, water and almond extract in a medium bowl; beat until smooth. Transfer frosting into small bowls and tint with food coloring. Spread onto cooled cookies.

Sugar Cookies
2 18-oz. pkgs. refrigerated
    sugar cookie dough
assorted cookie cutters
drinking straw (optional)
assorted candies and sprinkles

Roll out the dough to ¼-inch thickness. Cut out with cookie cutters (for cookie ornaments, before baking, use the straw to make a hole in each cookie for hanging). Place on ungreased baking sheets and bake at 350 degrees for 5 to 7 minutes or until golden. Decorate with frosting, candies and sprinkles. Makes 36 to 40.

Ribbon Chain

For paper chains all grown up, use ribbons instead of paper strips. Just loop the ribbons together and glue the ends with fabric glue. Layer ribbons for more color and texture.

Family Photo Ornaments

Gather up your cardstock, scrapbook paper, stickers, rub-on letters and other papercrafting supplies for an evening of family fun. Dress up family photos with festive cardstock and scrapbook paper backgrounds and frames (use foam dots to give some of the items dimension). Add ribbon hangers.

Welcome Home

At Christmastime, "home" is the sweetest word of all! When friends & family arrive at your house, you'll want them to see decorations that are really special. Getting this charming look is as easy as folding a fat quarter of vintage fabric and displaying cherished ornaments. Try these festive ideas to see how fast your home can extend a warm & cozy welcome!

Fat Quarter Napkins
(shown on page 17)

To make coordinating napkins, hem the sides of purchased fat quarters (or surprise your loved ones with some of their old favorite prints). Tie twill tape around each folded napkin and hot glue Christmas balls to the back of the knot.

Place Mats
(also shown on page 16)

These red & white place mats will conjure up sweet memories of Grandma's kitchen. Matching the short ends, fold a tea towel in half (our towel is 19"x28"). Sew a button at each corner...how simple!

Table Centerpiece
Never leave burning candles unattended.

For a centerpiece that will draw everyone to the table, knot twill tape around a pillar candle and place it in an oversized glass footed vase. Fill in around the candle with faux raspberries. Place fresh greenery around the vase and add red berry sprigs and glittered snowflakes to reflect the warm glow.

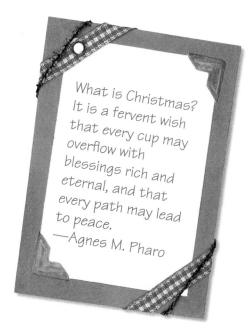

Tiered Ornament Display
• floral wire
• fresh greenery
• tiered wooden display
• vintage ornaments
• assorted ribbons
• faux red berries
• glittered snowflakes

Just a handful of vintage ornaments will inspire a tree-full of memories with this clever display. Wire greenery sprigs together to form a wreath to fit around each tier. Wire ornaments to the wreaths and tie a few to the center post with ribbon. Fill in with faux berries and glittered snowflakes for added sparkle.

Hanging Basket Arrangement

Everyone will feel like family when greeted with this welcoming arrangement. Faux red and green berries accent twigs and greenery in a whitewashed basket. Dangle a glittered snowflake from a brass label holder. Glue red and cream twill tape over the back of the holder and add a message with rub-on letters. Glue red twill tape around the basket, leaving a streamer at the front. Glue the label holder on top.

Chairback Wreaths

To "spruce" up your wooden chairs, use red twill tape to tie wired greenery-sprig wreaths to the chairbacks. Hang glittered snowflakes from the tape and glue cream twill tape with rub-on messages to the snowflakes.

Tea Towel Pillow

Matching right sides and leaving an opening for stuffing, sew two tea towels together; turn right side out. Stuff with fiberfill or a pillow form, sew the opening closed and add buttons at the corners for a charming accent pillow...in minutes!

sweet dreams.

Vintage Pillow

For a pillow that's sure to add a cozy touch to your room, cut a 19" square from a vintage or reproduction tablecloth or quilt piece and a 19" square backing. Matching right sides and leaving the bottom open for stuffing, sew the squares together; turn right side out. Insert an 18" square pillow form and sew the bottom closed. Beginning at the center back of the pillow, insert a needle through a button, the pillow and a button at the front. Take the needle back through the front button, pillow and back button. Pull the thread tightly and tie at the back to tuft.

Polka-Dot Christmas

Want a playful holiday theme that really hits the spot? Perky polka dots will spread cheer from table to tree! Use lighthearted hues to fashion a fast table runner, create a cluster of candlesticks and whip up plenty of tags and packages. Hang happy tags in the branches of the tree, and place pleasant presents on a dotted tree skirt. Now you have a way to tickle everyone's fancy, and maybe their funny bones, with your newfangled, polka-dot Christmas!

Polka-Dot Table Runner

- red flannel
- paper-backed fusible web
- red thread
- scraps of green and white flannel
- white pom-pom fringe
- ¹⁄₂"w green striped ribbon
- clear nylon thread

Add a spot of whimsy to your holiday tablescape with this cheery runner. Adding 1" for hems, cut a red flannel runner. Fuse all edges ¹⁄₂" to the wrong side. Fuse, then *Blanket Stitch* (page 128) green and white flannel circles to the runner. Sew the fringe and ribbon along the long edges with nylon thread.

Spool Candleholders

(shown on pages 22 and 23)
Never leave burning candles unattended.

Turn antique wooden spools into yuletide candleholders. Paint the spools with acrylic paints, adding stripes and dots as you like. Lightly sand for a slightly worn look. (You may need to trim the bottoms of your candles to fit the spool openings.)

Tag Ornaments

Spread holiday cheer with playful cardstock and scrapbook paper tag ornaments (patterns on page 134). Layer tags if you wish and embellish them with punched cardstock circles and die-cut messages (use foam dots to give some of the circles and letters dimension). Knot ribbon through holes punched in the tags and attach them with clothespins to a tree, wreath, garland or gift.

Polka-Dot Gift Boxes

Make your gifts oh-so cheery! Gather rolls of white paper for wrapping the gifts, glue on circles punched from painted cardstock and top the packages off with jumbo twill tape. Instead of using gift tags, make *Tag Ornaments* and clip them on the twill tape with clothespins.

Polka-Dot Tree Skirt

- 1½ yds of 60"w red flannel
- string
- fabric marking pen
- thumbtack
- paper-backed fusible web
- red thread
- ½ yd each of 44"/45"w green and white flannel
- 4½ yds white pom-pom fringe
- 4½ yds of ½"w green striped ribbon
- clear nylon thread
- three 2½" dia. self-covered buttons

1. Cut a 52" red flannel square. Follow *Making a Fabric Circle* on page 133 and use a 25" string measurement for the outer cutting line. Remove the tack and use a 2" string measurement for the inner cutting line.

2. Cut through all flannel layers along the drawn lines. Unfold the skirt and cut a front opening from the outer edge to the center opening.

3. Fuse, then *Blanket Stitch* (page 128) green and white flannel circles to the skirt.

4. Press the outer skirt edge ½" to the wrong side. Sew the fringe and ribbon along the outer edge with nylon thread.

5. Press the front and center openings ½" to the wrong side.

6. For the button loops, cut three 1½"x8" red flannel strips. Matching wrong sides and long edges, press each strip in half. Unfold the strip. Press the long edges to the center, refold the strip and sew the long edges together. Pin the loops to the wrong side along the front opening of the skirt.

7. For the front placket, matching right sides and long edges, fold a 4½"x23" green flannel piece in half and sew the short edges together. Turn right side out and pin to the front opening behind the button loops. Sew along the front and center openings, catching the placket and loops. Clip the curves.

8. Cover the buttons with green and white flannel and sew them along the front opening across from the loops.

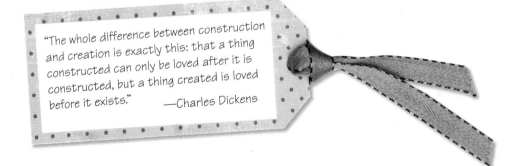

"The whole difference between construction and creation is exactly this: that a thing constructed can only be loved after it is constructed, but a thing created is loved before it exists."
—Charles Dickens

Polka-Dot Stocking

- 1 yd of 44"/45"w red flannel
- paper-backed fusible web
- red thread
- scraps of green and white flannel
- 1/2 yd white pom-pom fringe
- 1/2 yd of 11/2"w red and white polka-dot ribbon
- 11/4 yds of 1/2"w green striped ribbon
- clear nylon thread

Match right sides and use a 1/2" seam allowance unless otherwise indicated.

1. Enlarge the pattern on page 135 to 228%. Use the pattern and cut four stocking pieces (two in reverse for the stocking and lining backs) from red flannel.

2. Fuse, then *Blanket Stitch* (page 128) green and white flannel circles to one stocking piece for the front.

3. Leaving the top open, sew the stocking front and back together. Sew the remaining pieces together with a 3/4" seam for the lining. Turn the stocking right side out and place the lining inside. Baste the top edges together.

4. For the cuff, matching wrong sides and long edges, press a 71/2"x14" red flannel piece in half; unfold. Starting with the fringe at the fold and sewing through one layer only, layer and sew the fringe and ribbons to the cuff with nylon thread as shown (make sure this will be on the outside of the cuff when finished).

5. Matching the short edges, fold the cuff in half. Sew the short edges together and turn right side out. Matching wrong sides and raw edges, refold the cuff with the fringe on the outside.

6. For the hanger, fold an 81/2" green ribbon length in half. Matching raw edges, pin the folded ribbon along the seam on the fringe side of the cuff. Matching the raw edges and the cuff seam to the heel-side stocking seam, place the cuff in the stocking. Sew the cuff to the stocking along the raw edges. Turn the cuff to the outside.

Simply Stenciled

The Country Friends just barely remember when the sights of Christmas included playful window scenes created with canned "snow." This year, Holly discovered the nostalgic trend was back in fashion, so she hurried to create some stencils. Her windows looked so pretty that she decided to keep on stenciling! Holly's home was soon filled with frosty stockings, ornaments, a tree skirt and a bright banner. She even made a calendar to count down the days until Santa sees this new-again stenciled Christmas! Instructions for the Window Stencils and Advent Calendar begin on page 110.

Christmas Banner

(shown on page 28)
- red and white felt
- fabric glue
- white rickrack
- snowflake punch
- Stencil supplies (page 110)

Refer to Stencils (page 110) before you begin.

Put your happy holiday wishes on display. Cut a red felt banner; then, add ³/₄" all around and cut a white felt banner. Sew the red banner to the center of the white and glue rickrack over the seam.

Use a computer to print "Merry Christmas" and enlarge it to fit your banner. Using the small and medium snowflake patterns (page 137), the punch and the enlarged words, stencil the designs onto the banner.

Stenciled Stockings

- ³/₈ yd red felt for each
- ¹/₈ yd white felt for each
- fabric glue
- white rickrack
- Stencil supplies (page 110)
- white embroidery floss
- white sequins
- silver jingle bells

Refer to Stencils (page 110) before you begin. Match wrong sides and use a ¹/₄" seam allowance.

1. For each stocking, enlarge the pattern on page 136 to 146%. Use the enlarged pattern and cut two stockings (one in reverse) from red felt. Cut two 3"x13¹/₂" cuff pieces from white felt.

2. Leaving the top open, sew the stockings together. Glue rickrack over the seam.

3. Choose from the patterns on page 137 and stencil the designs onto the stocking (we enlarged our Santa to 136%). Add stitched floss-and-sequin snowflakes.

4. Stack and sew the cuff pieces together along the bottom long edge. Matching short edges, fold the cuff in half. Sew the short edges together; then, matching the open edges, sew the cuff to the stocking.

5. For the hanger, match long edges and fold a 1"x6¹/₂" red felt strip in half; sew the long edges together. Glue rickrack to the hanger. Sew the bell and hanger to the cuff.

Give and take makes good friends.
—SCOTTISH PROVERB—

Stenciled Tree Skirt

- 1¹/₈ yds red felt
- string
- fabric marking pen
- thumbtack
- 1¹/₈ yds white felt
- fabric glue
- white rickrack
- Stencil supplies (page 110)

Refer to Stencils (page 110) before you begin.

1. With this tree skirt, Santa will know right where to park the gifts. For the skirt, cut a 38" red felt square. Follow *Making a Fabric Circle* on page 133 and use an 18" string measurement for the outer cutting line. Remove the tack and use a 2" string measurement for the inner cutting line.

2. For the trim, repeat Step 1 with a 40" white felt square, using a 19", then 16" string measurement for the cutting lines.

3. Cut through all felt layers along the drawn lines. Unfold the skirt and the trim. Cut a back opening in the skirt from the outer edge to the center opening. Cut an opening in the trim. Save the leftover felt from the trim for use on other projects.

4. Sew the trim along the outer edge of the skirt and glue rickrack over the seam.

5. Enlarge the sleigh pattern on page 137 to 246%. Stencil the enlarged sleigh and the small and medium snowflake patterns (page 137) onto the skirt.

"There is nothing higher, stronger, more wholesome and useful for life in later years than some good memory, especially a memory connected with childhood, with home."

—Fyodor Dostoevsky

Santa's Sleigh Ornament

- tracing paper
- white felt
- red felt
- Stencil supplies (page 110)
- white embroidery floss
- white sequins
- fabric glue
- white rickrack
- red cord
- 1/4" dia. hole punch
- silver jingle bell

Refer to Stencils (page 110) before you begin.

1. Use the pattern on page 138 and cut two ornaments from white felt and one center from red felt.
2. Stencil the sleigh pattern (page 137) onto the center piece (only 2 reindeer will fit). Add a stitched floss-and-sequin snowflake. Sew the top and bottom of the center piece to one ornament. Stack and sew the ornaments together. Glue on rickrack.
3. Thread a knotted cord loop through a hole punched in the top of the ornament and glue the knot at the back. Sew a sequin and the bell to the bottom of the ornament.

Felt Ball Ornament

- tracing paper
- red and white felt
- Stencil supplies (page 110)
- white embroidery floss
- white sequins
- fiberfill
- silver jingle bell
- red cord
- fabric glue
- large red and white beads

Refer to Stencils (page 110) before you begin.

1. Use the pattern on page 138 and cut 3 red and 3 white felt wedges.
2. Stencil a small snowflake pattern (page 137) onto each red wedge. Add stitched floss-and-sequin snowflakes.
3. Alternating colors and leaving one seam open for stuffing, use a 1/4" seam allowance to sew the wedges together along the side edges. Stuff the ornament and sew the opening closed.
4. Add the bell at the bottom and a beaded hanger at the top.

Santa Sign Ornament

Refer to Stencils (page 110) before you begin.

A sure reminder to believe in Santa, this jolly sign doubles nicely as a package tie-on or door hanger. Stencil the Santa and small snowflake patterns (page 137) onto a 4½"x6½" red felt piece and add stitched floss-and-sequin snowflakes. Stack and sew the sign onto another same-size felt piece. Add rickrack, bells and sequins. Finish the sign with a felt and rickrack hanger glued to the back.

THE BEST THING ABOUT THE FUTURE IS THAT IT COMES ONLY one day at a time. -ABRAHAM LINCOLN-

DEC. 24
one more day!

Square Card Table Cover

(shown on page 34)

- red felt
- square card table
- fabric glue
- green jumbo rickrack
- tracing paper
- green faux leather
- 1/8" dia. hole punch
- craft knife and cutting mat
- eight 7/8" dia. buttons

1. Cut a felt square 11" larger than the tabletop. Glue rickrack along the edges.
2. Center the square on the tabletop. Pinch the corners together to form pleats and pin in place.
3. Using the pattern on page 144, cut four faux leather strips. Cut the holes and slits as marked.
4. Fasten the strips to buttons sewn to each side of the pleats.

Playing Card Tray

Instructions are on page 112.

Score Pad

Stack score cards cut from white paper on a same-size cardstock backing. Fold a faux leather strip in half and punch two holes through both layers. Punch matching holes in the score pad. Fold the leather over the top of the score pad and tie twill tape through the holes. To complete, glue a wavy-edged cardstock strip to the back edge of a striped paper strip and glue to the back edge of the leather on the front of the pad. Add rub-on letters.

Game-Piece Bags

For each of these quick bags, sew a felt tube; then, sew one end closed and turn. Tie the bag closed with twill tape or make a flap by cutting away the top edge at the front and the corners at the back of the bag. Fasten a faux leather closure (pattern on page 144) to buttons sewn to the bag and flap. Make a scrapbook paper tag and add rub-on letters. Tie the tag onto the bag with twill tape.

You can find the snack mix recipe on page 112.

Spiced Cider
The aroma is fantastic!

2 qts. apple cider
¼ c. brown sugar, packed
½ t. whole allspice
1 t. whole cloves

1 cinnamon stick
¼ t. salt
dash nutmeg
1 orange, cut in wedges

Prepare cider using a large automatic coffee maker. Substitute the cider for water. Place remaining ingredients in coffee basket with filter and brew. Makes two quarts.

— Pat Akers

Basket Liner
- paper for pattern (newspaper or kraft or butcher paper works well)
- basket
- tape
- striped fabric
- ⁷/₈"w fusible web tape

Fabric-lined baskets are handy for corralling your game-night entertainment. They make great gifts too!

1. To make a pattern, drape one length of paper over and into the basket horizontally, adding a 4" overhang to each end. Cut or fold the paper to fit inside the basket.
2. Repeat vertically across the first piece. Cut to fit. Tape the two pieces together to form a cross.
3. Arrange the pattern on the wrong side of the fabric. Adding ½" to each side for the seam allowance, cut out the fabric liner. Matching right sides, sew the corners together. Turn under and fuse a 1" hem along the top of the liner.

All the Creatures were Stirring

'Twas the night before Christmas, when all through the house, ALL the creatures were stirring, including the mouse! In the kitchen, a Spotty look-alike seems to play "tag" with a little gray mouse and a bewhiskered feline. From the dog dish tree stand to the mischievous kitty topper, pet-themed decorations fill the tree. Wouldn't your canine pal welcome the buckets of treats? Turn the page to find photo frames and framed ornaments that will show off your furry friends to perfection.

Spotty, Mouse, Kitty and Tabletop Tree Stand instructions are on pages 113-114.

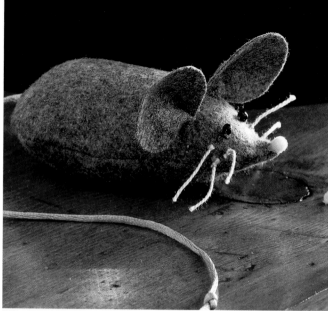

Mouse
Instructions are on page 114.

Luggage Tag Ornaments
Luggage tags are a quick & simple way to give your furry friends places of honor on the Christmas tree (they make fun package tie-ons too)…just slide photos inside and you're done. We removed the straps from our luggage tags and used them as mini collars for our *Kitty I.D. Tag Ornaments*, then replaced them with ball chain hangers.

Dog Bone Ornaments
Fido won't be able to wait to get his paws on these ornaments when he finds out there's a surprise inside…they squeak! To make each ornament, use the pattern on page 143 and cut 2 bones from fabric. Tuck the ends of a ribbon or trim hanger between the right sides of the bones and sew them together, leaving an opening for stuffing. Turn right side out. Stuff with fiberfill, place a pet toy squeaker inside and sew the opening closed.

Pet Silhouette Ornaments
These ornaments make the sweetest Christmas keepsakes for pet lovers. Use the patterns on page 143, or for silhouettes of your own pets, trace images from photos and transfer them onto cream ball ornaments. Paint the designs with black glass paint.

Pet Photo Frame

Personalize a display of your favorite four-legged friend. Glue pieces cut from a leather collar to a framed picture of your pet. Add a bell or metal tag to the collar. Stamp your pal's name on the tag with StazOn® ink.

Kitty I.D. Tag Ornaments

- tracing paper
- craft knife and cutting mat
- mat board
- ¹/₁₆" dia. hole punch
- silver metallic acrylic paint
- paintbrush
- alphabet stamps
- black StazOn® ink pad
- clear dimensional glaze
- jump rings
- lanyard hooks
- jingle bells
- straps removed from luggage tags

These clever ornaments are oversized replicas of Kitty's metal I.D. tag. For each ornament, use the pattern on page 143 and cut a tag from mat board. Punch a hole at the top. Paint the tag silver. Stamp Kitty's name on the tag and paint the tag with glaze. Use a jump ring to attach the tag to a lanyard hook and add a bell. Attach the hook to a luggage tag strap.

CHRISTMAS PAPER FUN

...CARDS, TAGS and more!

Of all the merry sights of Christmas, it's the personal touches we remember best. That's why these paper designs are sure to become favorite keepsakes. Create a set of cookie-cutter ornaments or a dimensional snowflake for the tree. Gift tags, greeting cards, pretty packages and a colorful shadowbox display...these are just a few of the fun ways you can use papercrafts to say, "Happy Holidays!"

Instructions for the Snowflake Ornament and Package Embellishments are on page 115.

Gift Tags

Pull out all your papercrafting supplies and have fun making these clever gift tags. We bet you'll even come up with a few designs of your own.

No Peeking

For this tag-within-a-tag, cut small and large cardstock tags (patterns on page 152). Add a scrapbook paper pocket to the large tag and liven it up with ribbon and rickrack. Sand the small tag and make a matching nametag for the pocket. Add rub-on letters and tie ribbons, fibers and twine onto the tags. Tuck the small tag in the pocket.

From Your Wish List

This playful tag is ideal for someone special. Make a layered cardstock and scrapbook paper tag and scuff it up a little with sandpaper. Spell out the message with colorful stickers (use foam dots for dimension) and rub-on letters; then, tie ribbons and fiber onto the tag. A metal-rimmed vellum tag stamped with the date for gift opening makes this tag even more fun.

Don't Open Until December 25

This tag is for all of us who find it hard to wait for Christmas! Matching short ends, fold a sanded 3"x8" textured cardstock piece in half. Write a message on the inside back. Zigzag scrapbook paper to the front and add the message with stamps, pens, rub-on letters, scrapbook paper and foam dots. Add a star charm with a brad at the bottom left corner. Wrap embroidery floss and fiber around the front near the fold and knot the ends around the brad. Attach a star charm to a fun binder clip with a jump ring and clip it onto the tag. Tie ribbons and fiber through a hole punched in the top left corner.

Ornament Gift Card Holder

- craft glue
- scrapbook paper
- gift card
- tracing paper
- cardstock
- foam brush
- glitter
- rickrack
- 1/8" dia. hole punch
- rub-on letters
- silver cord

1. Gluing the ends at the back, wrap a scrapbook paper strip around the gift card.
2. Use the patterns on page 153 and cut an ornament, pocket, cap, stripes and tag from cardstock.
3. Glue stripes on the ornament and pocket. Apply a thin layer of glue to the cap and dot glue on the pocket. Apply glitter, allow to dry and shake off the excess.

4. Glue rickrack along the top of the pocket; then, leaving the top open, glue the outer edge of the pocket to the ornament. Glue a rickrack hanger to the ornament front; then, glue the cap to the ornament over the hanger ends.
5. Punch a hole in the tag. Apply rub-ons to the tag and gift card wrapper. Tie the tag to the hanger with cord and insert the wrapped gift card in the pocket.

Pocket Gift Card Holder

- craft glue
- cardstock
- gift card
- rub-on letters
- tracing paper
- 2" dia. circle punch
- colored chalk
- 2 1/2"w velvet ribbon
- 1/8" dia. eyelet and setter
- black fine-point permanent pen
- 1"w snowflake punch
- satin ribbon
- fibers
- photo corners

1. Gluing the ends at the back, wrap a cardstock strip around the gift card. Apply rub-ons to the gift card wrapper.
2. Use the patterns on page 154 and cut a cardstock pocket and slide-out card. Punch a cardstock tag. Chalk the edges of the shapes.
3. Fold the side, then bottom pocket flaps to the back and glue together where they overlap. Wrap velvet ribbon around the pocket and glue the ends at the back.
4. Set the eyelet in the tag. Write a greeting around the edge. Glue a punched velvet snowflake to the tag and the slide-out card. Use satin ribbon and fibers to attach the tag to the pocket.
5. Slide photo corners over the gift card corners and adhere to the slide-out card. Insert the slide-out card in the pocket.

Monogram Money Holder

- craft glue
- 3³/₄"x8¹/₂" white card with envelope
- assorted scrapbook papers
- rickrack
- craft knife and cutting mat
- textured cardstock
- colored chalk
- adhesive foam dots
- silver snowflake charm
- rub-on letters

Cover the inside and outside of the card with scrapbook papers. Layer and glue paper strips and rickrack on the front. Use a computer to print the monogram and cut the letter from the center of a 3" cardstock square. Chalk the cardstock edges, back the cardstock with scrapbook paper and adhere to the card front with foam dots. Glue the charm to the monogram. Cut a scrapbook paper pocket with a wavy top edge to fit the inside card back. Add a rub-on message and glue the pocket in place.

Stocking Stuffer Money Holder

- craft glue
- 3³/₄"x8¹/₂" white card with envelope
- assorted scrapbook papers
- tracing paper
- textured cardstock
- black fine-point permanent pen
- black rub-on letters

Cover the card front with scrapbook paper. Use the pattern on page 152 and cut a stocking, heel and toe from scrapbook papers. Glue the pieces together, glue the stocking to cardstock and cut the cardstock slightly larger. Draw stitches on the heel and toe. Glue the stocking to the card front. Use rub-ons to add the message on the card front and inside back. Glue a scrapbook paper pocket to the inside card front. Glue a cardstock strip with a rub-on message to the pocket.

Home for the Holidays Photo Card

Make family & friends feel at home for the holidays no matter where they are. Mat a photo of your home on a scalloped piece of textured cardstock and glue it to a 5"x7" cardstock or double-sided scrapbook paper piece. Mat a message sticker and adhere to the card with foam dots. Add twill tape, fibers, metal embellishments and a nametag to make it extra special; then, drop it in the mail in a 5¼"x7¼" envelope.

Joy Card

Instructions are on page 116.

Noel Card

Cover the outside of a blank purchased card with scrapbook paper. Layer and glue scrapbook paper strips on the front near the fold. Close the card and round the corners. Machine sew swirly lines on the card front. Use adhesive foam dots to adhere round letter stickers along a wavy ribbon length glued on the card front.

Believe Card

Glue a piece of scrapbook paper to the front of a blank purchased card. Accent a large "Believe" sticker with scalloped cardstock strips. Spell out the message with cardstock and alphabet stickers and rub-on letters applied to assorted sizes of layered scrapbook paper circles. Adhere 2 of the circles with adhesive foam dots.

Card Box

Shorten a friend's Christmas card shopping list...fill this box with Handmade Cards for giving.

- tracing paper
- textured cardstock
- spray adhesive
- striped and dotted scrapbook papers
- craft glue
- $^3/_4$"w twill tape
- 1" dia. circle punch
- embroidery floss
- $^1/_4$" dia. brads
- $^3/_8$" dia. jingle bell

1. Use the patterns on pages 148-149 (enlarge the back to 120%) and cut a box front and back from cardstock. Working in a well-ventilated area, use spray adhesive to cover the front with striped paper and the back with dotted paper.
2. Fold the pieces along the dashed lines. Gluing the tabs to the inside, assemble the box.
3. For the handle, glue the ends of a 14" twill tape length inside the box.
4. For the closure, punch three cardstock circles. Knot the center of a 16" floss length around a brad; then, attach a cardstock circle to the box flap with the brad. Glue another circle over the brad prongs. Attach the last circle to the box with another brad. Tie the bell onto the floss ends; then, wrap the floss around the brads to close.

Handmade Cards

JINGLE BELL POSTCARD

Glue a deckle-edged scrapbook paper piece to a 4"x6" textured cardstock piece. Tear a piece from Christmas word print scrapbook paper and adhere to the card with foam dots. Make a textured cardstock jingle bell (pattern on page 150), add a nametag and a ribbon hanger and adhere to the card with foam dots.

ENJOY THE HOLIDAY

The base for this card is a 4"x6" textured cardstock piece. Spell "Enjoy the Holiday" on vellum with rub-on letters and tape the corners to the cardstock. Stitch paper photo corners on one end. Fold and tape a paper strip around the other end. For the ribbon slide, write a message on a paper circle. Cut slits in the top and bottom of the circle and in the paper strip on the card front. Thread ribbon and embroidery floss through the slits in the circle, then through the card slits and knot at the front. Glue a ribbon hanger to the card back and add a paper clip just for looks.

VERY MERRY CARD

For the base, glue scrapbook paper to a 3$\frac{3}{4}$"x6" cardstock piece. Make a 3$\frac{1}{2}$"x4$\frac{3}{4}$" scrapbook paper center flap and a 3$\frac{1}{2}$"x3$\frac{5}{8}$" layered scrapbook paper top flap. Fold the top edges of the flaps $\frac{3}{4}$" to the front; unfold. Staple the flaps, along with folded ribbons, to the base. Write and stamp messages on each layer of the card and add a cardstock heart with a foam dot. On the top flap, add a paper clip, staple a ribbon tab to the back and tie on a tiny jingle bell with embroidery floss. Add a knotted ribbon length to the base.

rick·rack and
ribbon!

Paper Bag Album

Scuff up two red lunch-size paper bags with sandpaper. Zigzag two sides of each bottom bag flap in place for extra pockets. Alternating ends, stack the bags; then, fold them in half. Leaving 1" on each side of the center fold undecorated, make album pages and glue or sew them to the album. For the spine, overlapping $1/2$" on the front, fold a $1^1/2$"-wide textured cardstock strip over the fold and zigzag in place. Make a front cover and glue it to the album. Add extra photos, trims and embellishments to the album as you like. Make pull-out pages to fit in the open bag ends or pockets.

from Hand to Heart

Nothing gets us in the Christmas spirit better than giving gifts! And doesn't the giving seem even more fun when you make the presents yourself? This assortment of ideas to share has something for everyone. Make an office organizer from felt that's sure to be appreciated. Play Santa's helper and create a gift wrap supply organizer, cover clothes hangers with vintage linens or add ribbon to a boxed set of photo albums. Just turn the pages to see more of these thoughtful projects. They're so exciting, you may have trouble keeping your plans secret!

Flocked Candle Box instructions are on page 116.
Motif Scrap Afghan instructions begin on page 117.

Hinged Frame with Ornament

- 2 same-size white photo frames with glass removed
- two 1" hinges
- screwdriver
- buttons
- craft glue
- adhesive foam dots
- patterned and solid scrapbook papers
- vellum tape
- vellum Christmas quote
- mica glitter
- papier-mâché ornament
- cream rickrack
- ⅛" dia. hole punch
- ribbon

Share a message of good tidings with this clever display. Connect the frames with the hinges. Adhere buttons to the frame corners with glue and foam dots. Cover one of the frame backings with patterned paper (discard the other backing). Tape the quote to solid paper and attach it to the frame backing with foam dots. Insert the backing in one frame.

Glue glitter on the top and bottom sections of the ornament and rickrack around the middle. Make a paper tag and add a button. Tie a ribbon hanger through the ornament and tag. Glue one ribbon end to the top back of the empty frame.

Boxed Photo Albums

Make a purchased boxed photo album set a more personal gift by fusing layered ribbons onto the box and albums. Add album labels in metal holders. To get an album started, mat a few special photos with coordinating colors of cardstock, attach photo corners and adhere the photos to the pages along with vellum and cardstock labels.

Egg Cup Pin Cushion

- green paint
- paintbrush
- egg cup
- brown embroidery floss
- 7½" tan wool felt square
- polyester fiberfill
- extra-strength craft glue
- 2" and 2½" dia. circle templates
- 3"x15" pink wool felt piece
- light blue rickrack
- tracing paper
- scrap of green wool felt
- sand

1. Paint the egg cup. Sew brown *French Knots* (page 128) at the center of the tan felt. Stuff the felt with fiberfill and tie closed with floss. Glue the bottom of the cushion in the cup.

2. For the inner row of petals, cut two 2" diameter pink felt circles in half. Cut four 2½" diameter circles in half for the remaining two rows. Overlapping for a rose petal look, glue the straight edge of the petals to the cushion, tucking the bottom row of petals in the cup. Glue rickrack around the cup.

3. For the needle sharpener, use the pattern on page 147 and cut two green felt leaves. Matching right sides and leaving an opening for turning, sew the leaves together. Turn right side out, fill with sand and sew the opening closed. Sew a vein along the center of the leaf and glue the leaf to the cup.

Flower Brooch

This happy little flower would make a great gift for a teacher, friend or secret pal. Use the pattern on page 152 and cut an illustration board backing and a slightly larger dark green wool felt backing; glue together. Cut stem/leaf and flower pieces from scraps of wool felt. Sew or glue buttons on the flower. Glue the flower, stem/leaf and a pin back to the backing. For a friend who doesn't wear jewelry, make it a magnet instead. Simply substitute a round magnet for the pin back.

Embellished Knitting Needles

These colorful needles will add cheer to a friend's craft area and they're simple to make! Lightly sand the tops of bamboo knitting needles; then, paint them with acrylic paints, adding stripes, zigzags and dots. Brush clear dimensional glaze over the painted areas. Top off the needles with glued-on felt beads.

Knitting Tote
Instructions begin on page 120.

Mommy & Me PJ's and Granny Square Slippers
Instructions for the Mommy & Me PJ's (with totes) and
Granny Square Slippers are on pages 122-125.

Gift Wrapping Organizer

- clear nylon thread
- 9¹/₂"x19¹/₄" felt piece
- ¹/₂ yd of 44"/45"w print fabric for backing and binding
- 8¹/₂" length of ³/₈" dia. dowel
- hankie
- linen tablecloth
- 6³/₄"x9¹/₂" fabric pieces for the front and back of each pocket (cut 6)
- buttons
- red embroidery floss

Vintage-look fabrics give this organizer old-time charm. Use a ¹/₄" seam allowance.

1. Sew the felt piece along the top and bottom edges to the wrong side of a same-size backing piece. To keep the organizer from drooping, make a dowel pocket by sewing 2" from the top edge and insert the dowel.

2. For the pocket front trims, cut two edges from the hankie and a corner from the tablecloth. Sew each trim along the top of a pocket front. Fold the top edge to the back (just for fun, fold the hankie pockets at a slant). Add buttons and decorative stitches to the pocket fronts.

3. Sew each pocket front to a pocket back piece along the sides (See Fig. 1 on page 116).

4. Using the photo as a guide, match right sides and sew the pockets together. Match wrong sides and sew the pockets to the backing along the outer edges.

5. For the binding, cut a 2"x9¹/₂" and a 2"x87" strip of print fabric (this will need to be pieced). Matching wrong sides and long edges, press each strip in half; then, unfold the strip. Press the long edges to the center and refold the strip. Sandwiching the organizer in the fold of the binding, sew the short binding strip to the top of the organizer. Center and sew the long binding strip to the bottom and sides of the organizer, mitering the corners. Continue sewing the long ends of the binding together and use them as ties. Fold the tie ends 1" to the back and add buttons to each.

Velvet Jewelry Pouch

- white waxed transfer paper
- blue-green velvet fat quarter
- red, green and ecru embroidery floss
- cotton fat quarter
- $1/8$"w ecru silk ribbon

Any woman will feel pampered when given this timeless pouch. Refer to Embroidery Stitches on pages 128-129 before beginning.

1. Enlarge the pattern on page 151 to 160%. Slide a sheet of transfer paper between the pattern and the velvet, with the waxed side toward the velvet. Transfer the pattern to the velvet.
2. Follow the Stitching Diagram on page 151 to embroider the velvet. Cut out the circle along the drawn line. Cut a cotton circle the same size.
3. Matching right sides and leaving an opening for turning, sew the circles together. Turn right side out. Press, cotton side up; then, sew the opening closed. Topstitch around the edge.
4. Using the ribbon and beginning and ending on the velvet side, work a *Running Stitch* through both layers around the edge of the circle. Knot both ribbon ends. Pull the ribbon and tie in a bow to close the pouch.

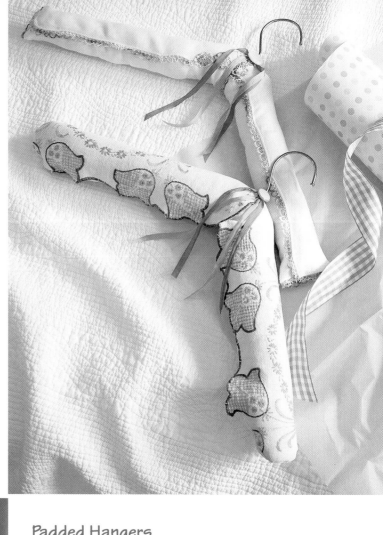

Padded Hangers

- fabric glue
- batting
- wooden hangers
- kraft paper
- linens with decorative edging
- $1/4$"w silk ribbons
- buttons

These hangers are so nice, no one will want to cover them up! Wrap and glue batting around each hanger. Draw around each half of the padded hanger separately (excluding the hook) on kraft paper to make patterns for the cover. Add enough of an allowance to the patterns for the decorative linen edges to overlap the raw edges and for the covers to overlap at the center of the hanger. Cut out the patterns and use them to cut the linens. Wrap and glue the covers around the hanger. (For the embroidered floral hanger, we matched right sides and sewed the rounded ends together, then turned the cover right side out before gluing to the hanger.) Add ribbons and buttons to make the hangers extra pretty.

Appliquéd Bag

- hand-dyed wool felt
- red felt bag
- cranberry embroidery floss
- gold and pink glass beads

Add a whimsical touch with this beaded bouquet.

1. Enlarge the patterns on page 146 to 128%. Use the patterns and cut flowers and stems from felt.
2. Pin the shapes to the bag.
3. Work *Running Stitches* (page 129) to sew the stems and large flowers to the bag. Attach the small round flowers with *Straight Stitches*. Add gold and pink beaded highlights to the flower centers.

Painted Guest Towels

Give guests an extra-special welcome...surprise them with their very own towels. Use a computer to print their initials; then, use transfer paper to transfer them onto purchased towels. Mix acrylic paint with textile medium and paint the letters. Add rickrack around the bottom with fabric glue and you're ready to show some hospitality.

Just·Right Gifts from the Kitchen

Cranberry Cider Mix

Find a nice blend of flavors in this mix.

12 cinnamon sticks, broken
  into pieces
½ c. sweetened,
  dried cranberries

1 T. whole allspice
1 T. nutmeg
½ t. ground cloves

Mix together all ingredients. Store in an airtight container. Include instructions with gift. Makes about 1½ cups mix. Instructions: In a large saucepan, combine 2 quarts apple cider, one quart water and cranberry cider mix; heat until warm. Add 2 sliced oranges. Makes 3 quarts.

(Apple Bags instructions are on page 126.)

Gifts from the kitchen are twice as nice...you have fun cooking them up; the recipients have fun eating them up! Is there anything that could make this assortment of goodies even better? Yes! You'll find terrific tags, bow-tied boxes and plenty of other clever ways to present your Christmas treats. Just don't be surprised when these delicious gifts show up on next year's wish lists!

Chocolate-Wrapped Peppermint Cookies

The two-tone dough and chocolate jimmies give these cookies a festive look!

1½ c. powdered sugar
1 c. butter, softened
1 egg
2¾ c. all-purpose flour
½ t. salt
¼ c. baking cocoa
1 T. milk
⅓ c. chocolate jimmies
¼ t. peppermint extract
4 drops red food coloring

Combine powdered sugar, butter and egg; mix in flour and salt. Divide dough in half; place each half in a separate mixing bowl. Add cocoa and milk to one half; mix well. Add chocolate jimmies, peppermint extract and food coloring to the remaining half; mix well. Roll out chocolate dough into a 12"x6" rectangle on wax paper; set aside.

Shape peppermint dough into a 12-inch long roll; place to fit on chocolate dough rectangle. Wrap chocolate dough around peppermint dough, using wax paper; seal seam. Keep dough wrapped in wax paper and refrigerate until firm, at least 2 hours.

Remove wax paper; cut dough into ¼-inch thick slices. Arrange on ungreased baking sheets; bake at 375 degrees for 8 to 10 minutes. Cool on a wire rack. Makes 4½ dozen.

(Holly Tag instructions are on page 127.)

Chocolate-Raspberry Truffles

A wonderful melt-in-your-mouth candy!

3 c. chocolate chips, divided
2 T. whipping cream
1 T. butter
2 T. seedless raspberry jam

Combine 1½ cups chocolate chips, whipping cream and butter in a double boiler over low heat; stir until melted and smooth. Add raspberry jam; remove from heat and cool. Cover with plastic wrap and freeze for 20 minutes. Shape into one-inch balls and freeze until firm.

Melt remaining 1½ cups chocolate chips in a double boiler over low heat; using a toothpick, dip balls into melted chocolate. Place on wire racks; chill until set. Makes about 3 dozen.

Virginia Garrelts
Salina, KS

(Truffle Box instructions are on page 127.)

Gingerbread Cookie Canister

- scallop- and deckle-edged scissors
- red felt
- brown lightweight cardboard
- white acrylic paint
- paintbrush
- brown chalk and colored pencil
- craft glue
- ³⁄₈"w and 1¹⁄₂"w ribbons
- canister with lid
- scrapbook papers
- rub-on letters
- twine
- ¹⁄₈" dia. hole punch
- adhesive foam dot

Cut a 3¹⁄₂" diameter scalloped felt circle and a 3" diameter deckle-edged cardboard "cookie." Paint "gingerbread cookies" on the cardboard cookie and color with chalk and the pencil. Gluing the ends at the front, wrap the wide ribbon around the center of the canister. Glue the felt circle to the front. Wrap and glue the narrow ribbon around the canister and glue the cardboard cookie to the felt circle. Make a layered scrapbook paper tag and add a name with rub-ons. Knot twine through a hole punched in the top and adhere the tag to the lid with the foam dot.

Decorated Gingerbread Cookies

Nothing says "the holidays" like gingerbread, and these pretty cookies will make someone very happy!

1¹⁄₂ c. light molasses
1 c. brown sugar, packed
²⁄₃ c. cold water
¹⁄₃ c. shortening
6 c. all-purpose flour
2 t. baking soda
¹⁄₂ t. salt
1 t. allspice
1 t. ground ginger
1 t. ground cloves
1 t. cinnamon

Mix first four ingredients together until thoroughly combined. Sift together dry ingredients and stir into molasses mixture. Chill dough overnight.

When ready to bake, roll dough to ¹⁄₄-inch thickness and use a 3¹⁄₄-inch round cookie cutter to cut out cookies. Place on lightly greased baking sheets; bake at 350 degrees for 15 minutes. Decorate with icing. Makes 3 dozen.

Decorated Gingerbread Cookie Royal Icing:

2¹⁄₄ c. powdered sugar
1¹⁄₂ T. meringue powder
2 to 3 T. warm water
¹⁄₂ t. almond extract

Beat all ingredients with an electric mixer until stiff. Spoon icing into a pastry bag fitted with a small round tip. Pipe snowflake design onto tops of cookies.

Chocolate-Peanut Butter Cookies
Two favorite flavors combine for a great-tasting cookie.

$1/2$ c. butter or margarine, softened
$1/2$ c. creamy peanut butter
1 c. powdered sugar
$3/4$ c. brown sugar, packed
1 egg
1 t. vanilla extract
1 c. all-purpose flour
$1/2$ c. baking cocoa
$1/4$ t. salt

In a large bowl, beat butter, peanut butter and sugars until fluffy. Add egg and vanilla; beat until smooth. In a small bowl, combine flour, cocoa and salt. Add dry ingredients to butter mixture; stir until a soft dough forms. Cover dough and chill 2 hours.

On a lightly floured surface, use a floured rolling pin to roll out dough to $1/4$-inch thickness. Use $1 1/2$-inch high cookie cutters or patterns on page 144 to cut out cookies. Place on greased baking sheets. Bake at 375 degrees for 7 to 9 minutes or until edges are firm. Transfer cookies to a wire rack to cool. Store in an airtight container. Makes about 11 dozen.

Divided Cookie Box
- $4^3/8$"x$4^7/8$" cookie box with flap lid (we found ours in the cake decorating section at a local craft store)
- craft glue
- scrapbook paper
- red and yellow textured cardstock
- tracing paper
- mat board
- craft knife and cutting mat
- sandpaper
- red chalk
- alphabet stamps
- brown ink pad
- ribbon
- Chocolate-Peanut Butter Cookies
- foil cupcake liners

1. Trimming and folding the edges to the inside, cover the box lid with scrapbook paper. Glue red cardstock to the inside of the lid.

2. Use the pattern on page 144 and cut a star from mat board. Cover the star with yellow cardstock. Sand and chalk the edges and stamp "Merry Christmas" on the star. Glue the star to the lid. Tie ribbon into a bow around the lid at the fold and secure with a dot of glue.

3. For the dividers, matching long edges, fold a $3^5/8$"x$4^1/2$" red cardstock piece in half and cut a $5/8$" long slit in the center of the folded edge. Matching long edges, fold a $3^3/4$"x$4^1/8$" red cardstock piece in half and cut a $1^1/8$" long slit in the center of the unfolded edges. Cross and connect the dividers and place them in the box.

4. Stack the cookies in the liners inside the box.

If you enjoy putting a personal touch on gift packages, your friends probably do too. Why not invite the gang over for a Christmas crafting party so everyone can make bags, tags and boxes for their own food gifts? Send out a few of these creative invitations, and gather plenty of crafting supplies. And be sure to prepare a few of these yummy recipes for everyone to enjoy while they work. What fun!

Party Invitations

- 5⅞"x7⅞" white flat cards with envelopes
- craft glue
- scrapbook papers
- alphabet stickers
- rub-on letters
- deckle- and large scallop-edged scissors
- white vellum
- square brads
- lightweight cardboard
- corner rounder
- ⅜" dia. silver jingle bells
- ¼"w red and ⅜"w green ribbons
- white and red cardstock
- sandpaper
- twine
- eyelets and setter

These festive invitations are mailable, but be sure to have them hand-cancelled.

1. For each invitation, cover the card with scrapbook paper.
2. For the pocket, spell the message with stickers and rub-ons on a 4⅞"x5⅛" deckle-edged vellum piece. Attach the vellum to a 5¾"x5⅞" scrapbook paper piece with brads. Glue a scalloped cardboard border along the right edge of the pocket. Glue the pocket to the outer edges only on the left side of the card. Round the card corners. Threading bells onto the red ribbon, tie layered ribbons around the card along the scalloped border; secure with glue.
3. For the tags, cut three 1¾"x6" white cardstock pieces. Glue torn scrapbook paper or sanded red cardstock to one end of each tag. Add the party information on the tags with rub-ons and round the corners. Knot ribbon and twine through eyelets attached to the tags.

Festive Cranberry Honey

This recipe makes enough to give several gifts.

3 16-oz. cans whole berry cranberry sauce
12-oz. jar orange marmalade
1½ c. honey

Place cranberry sauce and marmalade in a large microwave-safe bowl. Microwave on high 2 minutes or until melted. Stir in honey until well blended. Spoon into jars with lids. Store in the refrigerator. Serve with breads or use as a glaze for meat. Makes about 8 cups.

Honey Jars

Pick up small jelly jars by the boxfuls for party guests to fill and decorate for gift giving. Remove the ring and lid from each jar. Use double-sided tape to cover the lid with scrapbook paper. Replace the lid and ring on the jar. Fold and glue a green scrapbook paper piece in half. Cut holly leaves from the doubled paper (pattern on page 145). Pinch the bottoms of the leaves and connect them with a brad. Thread three red wooden beads onto green embroidery floss and tie onto the brad. Glue the leaves to the lid. Tie a ribbon bow around the jar neck.

Cellophane Bag Topper
- scrapbook papers
- craft glue
- scallop-edged scissors
- assorted ribbons
- tracing paper
- cardstock scrap
- message rubber stamp
- ink pad
- twine
- embroidery floss
- $1/16$" dia. hole punch
- $1/8$" dia. brads
- 5"x11$1/2$" cellophane bag filled with Dipped & Drizzled Pretzels
- $3/8$" dia. jingle bell

For the topper, match short edges and fold a 5"x6" scrapbook paper piece in half. Glue a 1"-wide scalloped scrapbook paper strip along one short edge for the front. Glue ribbon over the paper seam. Use the patterns on page 145 and make cardstock and scrapbook paper tags. Stamp a message on the small tag. Layer the tags and knot ribbons, twine and floss through holes punched in the tops. Attach the tags to the topper with a brad. Fold the top of the bag to the back and sandwich it in the fold of the topper. Punch holes through all layers at each end of the ribbon on the topper front. Attach brads through the holes to close the bag. Tie the bell to one brad with floss.

Dipped & Drizzled Pretzels
A pretty and tasty gift!

18 oz. white melting chocolate, divided
4 c. small pretzel twists
pink paste food coloring

Melt 12 ounces white chocolate in a double boiler. Dip pretzels in melted chocolate and place on wax paper to harden. Melt remaining 6 ounces white chocolate in a small saucepan and tint pink; drizzle over pretzels. Allow to harden. Store in an airtight container. Makes 5 cups.

Chewy Graham Popcorn
Snacks are always a welcomed gift!

10 c. popped popcorn
1¹/₂ c. golden raisins
2¹/₂ c. graham cracker cereal
1 c. mini marshmallows
1 c. chopped, dried dates
¹/₄ c. butter, melted
¹/₄ c. brown sugar, packed
2 t. cinnamon
¹/₂ t. ground ginger
¹/₂ t. nutmeg

Toss together first 5 ingredients; stir well. In a small bowl, combine remaining ingredients; stir into popcorn mixture. Pour mixture in a jelly-roll pan; bake at 250 degrees for 20 minutes, stirring after 10 minutes. Cool. Makes about 3 quarts.

Stamped Bags
(also shown on page 73)

Your party guests will appreciate the simplicity of this make-ahead gift packaging idea. Decorate lunch-size paper bags with Christmas stamps, acrylic paints, glue and glitter. Trim the tops of the bags with scallop-edged scissors. For each tag, stamp a design on white cardstock, sprinkle with glitter and cut out. Add a silver cord hanger through a hole punched in the top of the tag. Make a ribbon loop bow for each bag; then, tie separate ribbon lengths around the center for ties. Glue the tag hanger and the bow to the bag front. Thread the tie ends through holes punched through both layers near the top of the bag and knot at the back.

Recipe Cards

Chewy Graham Popcorn is so tasty, everyone will want the recipe, so why not send a recipe card home with each guest? For each card, type and print the recipe onto white vellum and tear away the bottom edge. Use vellum tape to adhere the vellum to an index card covered with scrapbook paper. Trim the bottom edge with large scallop-edged scissors and punch a hole in each scallop. Glue a scrapbook paper strip along the top edge and tie ribbons around the card.

A Farmhouse Dinner

The aroma of a country ham, the richness of pumpkin cake, mugs filled to the brim with warm spiced cider...if you've ever longed for an old-fashioned farmhouse dinner at Christmastime, here's the menu you'll want to serve! This meal is a delicious mix of traditional dishes with a few of the Country Friends' new favorites added. From the Celebration Cheese Balls to Granny's Sweet Potato Pie, you'll provide all the just-right flavors of the season.

Celebration Cheese Balls

Celebration Cheese Balls

This make-ahead snack is great when unexpected guests drop by. Keep one in the refrigerator...just in case.

2 8-oz. pkgs. cream cheese, softened
8-oz. pkg. shredded sharp Cheddar cheese
1 T. Worcestershire sauce
1/2 t. salt
1/4 t. celery salt
1 c. chopped pecans, toasted

Blend together first 5 ingredients. Cover and chill 3 hours; then, shape into two balls. Roll in pecans. Keep refrigerated until serving. Makes 8 to 10 servings.

Cheri Emery
Quincy, IL

Spinach-Pecan Salad

The combination of flavors in this salad makes it a favorite!

1 T. butter or margarine
1 T. brown sugar, packed
1/2 c. pecan halves
7-oz. pkg. baby spinach, washed
1 Granny Smith apple, thinly sliced
1/2 c. crumbled blue cheese
3 T. olive oil
2 T. white vinegar
1/8 t. salt
1/8 t. pepper

Melt butter and sugar in a small skillet over low heat, stirring constantly. Add pecan halves; cook 2 to 3 minutes, turning to coat. Remove coated pecans from skillet and cool on wax paper.

Toss spinach, apple, cheese and pecans in a serving bowl. Whisk oil, vinegar, salt and pepper; drizzle over salad, tossing gently to coat. Serves 4.

Spinach-Pecan Salad

Butternut Squash Soup

A creamy, flavorful soup that is perfect to start a holiday meal.

3-lb. butternut squash
8 carrots, peeled and cut
  into pieces
$2^{1}/_{2}$ c. chicken broth
$^{3}/_{4}$ c. orange juice
$^{1}/_{2}$ t. salt
$^{1}/_{2}$ t. ground ginger
$^{1}/_{2}$ c. whipping cream
Garnish: 2 T. finely
  chopped, toasted
  pecans and nutmeg

Cut squash in half lengthwise; remove seeds. Place squash, cut sides down, in a shallow pan; add hot water to pan to depth of $^{3}/_{4}$ inch. Cover with aluminum foil and bake at 400 degrees for 40 minutes or until tender; drain. Scoop out pulp; mash. Discard shell.

Cook carrots in boiling water 25 minutes or until tender; drain and mash.

Combine squash, carrots, chicken broth and next 3 ingredients in a bowl. Process half of mixture in a food processor or blender until smooth. Repeat procedure with remaining half of squash mixture.

Place puréed mixture in a large saucepan; bring to a simmer. Stir in cream; return to a simmer. Remove from heat.

To serve, ladle into individual bowls. Sprinkle with pecans and nutmeg. Makes 8 cups.

Melt-In-Your-Mouth Rolls

These rolls are the perfect accompaniment to any meal!

$^{3}/_{4}$ c. plus 1 t. sugar, divided
$^{1}/_{2}$ c. warm water
2 T. active dry yeast
1 c. butter-flavored shortening
1 c. boiling water
1 c. cold water
4 eggs, beaten
2 t. salt
8 c. all-purpose flour, divided
non-stick vegetable spray

Dissolve one teaspoon sugar in warm water; sprinkle yeast over it and set aside. Blend shortening and remaining $^{3}/_{4}$ cup sugar; stir in boiling water. Add cold water, yeast mixture, eggs and salt; mix well. Add flour, 4 cups at a time; mix well. Let dough rise for one hour.

Divide dough into thirds. Roll each third into a circle; cut into 12 wedges. Roll each wedge up crescent-roll style. Cover with plastic wrap that has been sprayed with non-stick vegetable spray; let rise another hour. Bake on ungreased baking sheets at 350 degrees for 15 to 18 minutes. Makes 3 dozen.

Jerilyn Anderson
Provo, UT

Homestyle Green Beans

This is a tasty way to serve fresh green beans.

2 lbs. green beans, trimmed
2 c. water
1 t. salt
$^{1}/_{3}$ c. butter or margarine
$1^{1}/_{2}$ T. sugar
1 t. dried basil
$^{1}/_{2}$ t. garlic powder
$^{1}/_{4}$ t. salt
$^{1}/_{4}$ t. pepper
2 c. halved cherry or grape
  tomatoes

Place beans in a Dutch oven; add water and salt. Bring to a boil; cover, reduce heat and simmer 15 minutes or until tender. Drain; keep warm.

Melt butter in a saucepan over medium heat; stir in sugar and next 4 ingredients. Add tomatoes and cook, stirring gently until thoroughly heated.

Pour tomato mixture over beans, and toss gently. Serve hot. Makes 8 servings.

Homestyle Green Beans

Corn Pudding

If you have it, try this dish using fresh sweet corn. Yum!

16-oz. can corn, drained
16-oz. can creamed corn
2 c. shredded Cheddar cheese
1 c. sour cream
8-oz. pkg. corn muffin mix
1/2 c. butter, melted
2 eggs, beaten

Combine all ingredients. Pour into a greased 11"x7" baking dish. Bake at 350 degrees for 20 to 25 minutes. Makes 6 servings.

Roasted Vegetables

Easy to assemble and bake while you are finishing other items for dinner.

1 1/2 lbs. sweet potatoes, peeled and cut into 1 1/2-inch pieces
3/4 lb. turnips, peeled and cut into 1 1/2-inch pieces
1 onion, peeled and cut into 1 1/2-inch wedges
6 cloves garlic, peeled
3 T. olive oil
1 T. rosemary, chopped
1 T. oregano or marjoram, chopped
1 t. salt

Combine first 5 ingredients in a large bowl; toss well. Place vegetables in a single layer in a large roasting pan or broiler pan. Bake at 450 degrees for 25 to 30 minutes or until vegetables are tender, stirring gently every 10 minutes. Stir in herbs and salt just before serving. Makes 6 servings.

Cider-Baked Ham

Cider-Baked Ham

On Christmas Eve, I baked this ham and took it, along with all the trimmings, to Grandpa's house for a surprise dinner. We had a lovely day together and a white Christmas too!

12 to 14-lb. cooked ham
whole cloves
2 c. apple cider
1 stick cinnamon
1 t. whole cloves
1/2 t. allspice
1/2 c. brown sugar, packed
1/2 c. honey

Place ham in a shallow roasting pan. Score diagonal lines in fat with the tip of a knife to form diamond shapes, being careful not to cut into meat. Stud each diamond with a whole clove. Combine apple cider, cinnamon, 1 teaspoon cloves and allspice in a small saucepan; heat to boiling. Cover and simmer for 5 minutes; pour over ham. Bake, uncovered, at 325 degrees, basting every 30 minutes with cider sauce for about 3 hours.

Remove ham from oven. Increase oven temperature to 400 degrees. Combine brown sugar and honey in a small saucepan. Cook over low heat, stirring until sugar is melted. Brush over top of ham.

Return ham to 400-degree oven. Bake 30 additional minutes, brushing the ham every 10 minutes with remaining honey mixture until brown and glistening and meat thermometer registers 160 degrees.

Remove from oven. Let stand 20 minutes before slicing. Makes 24 to 26 servings.

Kelly Hall
Butler, MO

Grace's Bourbon Balls

It doesn't take many ingredients to make this special treat.

1¼ c. pecans, finely chopped or
    ground
2½ c. vanilla wafers, crushed
    (12-oz. box makes 3 c.)
2 T. baking cocoa
2 T. dark corn syrup
⅓ c. bourbon
powdered sugar
2 T. baking cocoa
¼ c. powdered sugar

Combine first 5 ingredients and pinch together with hands. With powdered sugar on hands, roll into one-inch balls. Roll half the balls in powdered sugar again. Combine remaining 2 tablespoons cocoa and ¼ cup powdered sugar; roll remaining balls in cocoa mixture. Store in tins lined with wax paper.

Do not serve for at least 2 weeks. Great if frozen a month ahead. Makes about 41.

Lee Charrier

Holiday Apple & Cranberry Casserole

A fruit casserole is a nice addition to any meal.

3 c. apples, unpeeled and diced
    (hard or tart varieties)
2 c. cranberries
1 c. sugar
1 c. quick-cooking oats, uncooked
1 c. chopped pecans
½ c. brown sugar, packed
butter

Place the apples, cranberries and sugar in the bottom of a 13"x9" well-buttered casserole dish. Mix together the oats, pecans and brown sugar and sprinkle over the top of fruit. Dot the entire top with butter. Bake at 325 degrees for one hour. Makes about 8 servings.

Kathi Stein

Montana Winter Spiced Cider

It gets cold here in Montana…not just anything will warm you like this hug in a mug!

¾ c. brown sugar, packed
½ c. vanilla ice cream, softened
2 T. butter, softened
1 t. cinnamon
1½ gal. apple cider
Garnish: cinnamon

Combine the first 4 ingredients together in a blender; blend until smooth. Pour into a freezer-safe dish; cover and freeze several hours.

Heat apple cider thoroughly in a large saucepan; pour into serving mugs. Add one tablespoon frozen mixture to each mug; stir until melted. Sprinkle cinnamon on top. Makes 24 servings.

Linda Reynolds
Cut Bank, MT

Farmhouse Punch

A flavorful punch for any occasion.

46-oz. can apple juice
46-oz. can pineapple juice
12-oz. can frozen orange juice
    concentrate, thawed
2 qts. ginger ale

Combine apple juice, pineapple juice and orange juice until well blended. Add ginger ale and stir to mix. Makes 40 servings.

Granny's Sweet Potato Pie

It's just not the holidays without a sweet potato pie.

3 to 4 sweet potatoes
1½ c. sugar
2 eggs
1 t. cinnamon
1 T. vanilla extract
12-oz. can evaporated milk
2 9-inch pie crusts

Add sweet potatoes to a large saucepan, cover with water and bring to a boil. Continue to boil potatoes until tender. Drain water and set potatoes aside to cool.

When potatoes are cool enough to handle, remove peel and discard. Place potatoes in a large mixing bowl and beat on high speed with an electric mixer until smooth. Add sugar, mixing well, then add eggs, cinnamon and vanilla, blending thoroughly after adding each ingredient. Reduce mixer speed to low and add milk. Divide equally into unbaked pie crusts and bake at 425 degrees for 30 to 45 minutes. Makes 12 to 16 servings.

Pumpkin Cake Roll

Pumpkin Cake Roll

You will have people wanting another piece of this delicious dessert.

³/₄ c. all-purpose flour
2 to 3 t. pumpkin pie spice
1 t. baking powder
¹/₂ t. salt
3 eggs
1 c. sugar
²/₃ c. canned pumpkin
1 t. lemon juice
1 c. pecans or walnuts, finely
    chopped
powdered sugar

Combine flour, pumpkin pie spice, baking powder and salt. In a separate bowl, beat eggs on high speed with an electric mixer for 5 minutes. Gradually beat in sugar.

Stir in pumpkin and lemon juice. Stir in flour mixture. Spread in a greased and floured 15"x10"x1" pan. Sprinkle nuts on top. Bake at 375 degrees for 15 minutes.

Turn out on towel sprinkled with powdered sugar. Starting at narrow end, roll towel and cake together and let cool. Unroll. Spread filling over cake and reroll. Chill.

Serve hot Nutmeg Sauce over pumpkin cake roll, if desired. Serves 8 to 10.

Filling:
1 c. powdered sugar
6 oz. cream cheese, softened
4 T. butter
¹/₂ t. vanilla extract

Combine powdered sugar, cream cheese, butter and vanilla. Beat until smooth.

Nutmeg Sauce:
1 c. sugar
2 T. all-purpose flour
¹/₂ t. nutmeg
2 c. water
1 T. butter
1 T. white or cider vinegar

Combine sugar, flour and nutmeg in 2-qt. saucepan. Add water and stir while heating to a boil. Reduce heat and boil gently for 5 minutes. Stir frequently. Remove from heat and stir in butter and vinegar.

Lisa Murch

CHRISTMAS BRUNCH

It's Christmas morning! Offer your sleepyheads a selection of these delicious day-starters. You can awaken their festive spirits with a new twist on traditional breakfast fare, or serve up one of several meatless dishes. Better yet…recruit your family to prepare all these temptations while you sleep in!

Country Breakfast Skillet

Country Breakfast Skillet

All of your early morning favorites together!

16-oz. pkg. frozen hash browns, thawed
salt and pepper to taste
garlic powder to taste
6 to 8 eggs
1/3 c. milk
1/4 lb. cooked ham, chopped
1 to 2 tomatoes, chopped
4 to 6 green onions, thinly sliced
1 1/2 c. shredded Cheddar cheese

Cook hash browns according to package skillet directions. Season with salt, pepper and garlic powder; set aside.

Beat eggs with milk; add ham, tomatoes and onions. Over medium heat, stir egg mixture into hash browns; stir quickly to scramble. As the eggs begin to get firm, add cheese and continue to stir until eggs are cooked and set. Serve in 4 (6-inch) cast iron skillets, if desired. Makes 4 servings.

Natalie Roberge
Stillwater, MN

Blueberry-Croissant French Toast

A simple twist on a favorite breakfast classic.

1 c. half-and-half
2 eggs
$^1/_3$ c. sugar
$^1/_4$ c. milk
1 t. cinnamon
$^1/_4$ t. salt
8 T. blueberry preserves
4 croissants, sliced horizontally
$^1/_2$ c. butter
1 pt. blueberries
Garnish: maple syrup

Mix the first 6 ingredients together in a 13"x9" glass baking dish; whisk well and set aside.

Spread 2 tablespoons preserves on each of 4 croissant halves; top with remaining halves. Arrange croissants on top of egg mixture; turn to coat. Set aside until liquid is absorbed, about 45 minutes; turn often.

Melt butter in a 10" skillet over medium-high heat; add croissants. Heat until golden on both sides; transfer to serving plates.

Add blueberries to same skillet; heat thoroughly, about 3$^1/_2$ minutes. Spoon berries over croissants; garnish with maple syrup. Makes 4 servings.

Jo Ann

Sweet Fruit & Cream

Sweet Fruit & Cream

Yummy and healthy…what more could you ask for!

2 c. plain or vanilla yogurt
4 oz. cream cheese, softened
$^3/_4$ c. quick-cooking oats, uncooked
$^3/_4$ c. chopped pecans
$^1/_2$ c. strawberries, sliced
$^1/_2$ c. grapes, halved
$^1/_2$ c. flaked coconut
1 banana, sliced
1 apple, chopped
2 t. lemon juice
$^3/_4$ c. whipping cream
sugar to taste
Garnish: pecans and toasted coconut

Blend together yogurt and cream cheese. Beat at medium speed with an electric mixer for 2 minutes or until well blended. Stir in the oats, pecans, strawberries, grapes, coconut, banana, apple and lemon juice; set aside.

In a large, chilled bowl, combine whipping cream with sugar. Beat at medium-high speed with an electric mixer until soft peaks form; fold in fruit mixture. Garnish with pecans and coconut. Makes 8 servings.

Zoe Bennett
Columbia, SC

Garden-Fresh Egg Casserole

Fresh tomatoes and spinach turn this breakfast casserole into something extra special. I think it's perfect for overnight guests.

18 eggs, beaten
1$^1/_2$ c. shredded Monterey Jack cheese
1 c. buttermilk
1 c. cottage cheese
1 c. spinach, chopped
1 c. tomatoes, chopped
$^1/_2$ c. butter, melted
$^1/_2$ c. onion, grated

Mix all ingredients together; pour into a greased 13"x9" baking pan. Cover; refrigerate overnight.

Bake at 350 degrees for 50 minutes to one hour. Serves 8 to 10.

Anne Muns
Scottsdale, AZ

Tangy Cranberry Breakfast Cake
Three scrumptious layers!

2 c. all-purpose flour
1 1/3 c. sugar, divided
1 1/2 t. baking powder
1/2 t. baking soda
1/4 t. salt
2 eggs, divided
3/4 c. orange juice
1/4 c. butter, melted
2 t. vanilla extract, divided
2 c. cranberries, coarsely chopped
Optional: 1 T. orange zest
8-oz. pkg. cream cheese, softened

Combine flour, one cup sugar, baking powder, baking soda and salt in a large bowl; mix well and set aside.

Combine one egg, orange juice, butter and one teaspoon vanilla in a small bowl; mix well and stir into flour mixture until well combined. Fold in cranberries and then zest, if using. Pour into a greased 9" round springform pan and set aside.

Beat together cream cheese and remaining 1/3 cup sugar in a small bowl until smooth. Add remaining egg and remaining one teaspoon vanilla; mix well. Spread over batter; sprinkle with topping. Place pan on a baking sheet; bake at 350 degrees for 1 1/4 hours or until golden. Let cool on wire rack for 15 minutes before removing sides of springform pan. Serves 12.

Topping:
6 T. all-purpose flour
1/4 c. sugar
2 T. butter

Combine flour and sugar in a small bowl. Cut in butter with a fork until mixture resembles coarse crumbs.

Linda Hendrix
Moundville, MO

Pecan French Toast
This overnight, oven-baked French toast will win you raves!

1 loaf French bread, sliced
6 eggs
1 1/2 c. milk
1 1/2 c. half-and-half
1 t. vanilla extract
1 t. cinnamon
1/8 t. nutmeg

Arrange bread in a lightly greased 13"x9" baking pan; set aside.

Beat together remaining ingredients; pour over bread. Cover; refrigerate overnight.

Spread topping over mixture; bake at 350 degrees for 45 to 55 minutes. Let stand 5 minutes before serving. Serves 6 to 8.

Topping:
1 c. brown sugar, packed
1 c. chopped pecans
1/2 c. butter, softened
2 T. maple syrup

Mix all ingredients together.

Darcie Stearns
Rock Island, IL

Quiche-Me-Quick
The name may make you smile, but the taste will have you coming back for more!

1/2 c. butter
1/2 c. all-purpose flour
6 eggs, beaten
1 c. milk
16-oz. pkg. Monterey Jack cheese, cubed
2 c. cottage cheese
3-oz. pkg. cream cheese, softened
1 t. baking powder
1 t. salt
1 t. sugar

Melt butter in a saucepan; add flour. Cook and stir until smooth; beat in the remaining ingredients. Stir until well blended; pour into a greased 13"x9" baking pan. Bake at 350 degrees for 45 minutes. Serves 10 to 12.

Sandy Bernards
Valencia, CA

Pecan French Toast

Sweet Potato Biscuits

These taste great!

³/₄ c. sweet potatoes, cooked,
    peeled, mashed and chilled
½ c. butter, melted and cooled
¼ c. brown sugar, packed
½ c. milk
2 c. all-purpose flour
1½ t. baking powder
½ t. salt

In a large bowl, combine the sweet potatoes, butter and brown sugar. Stir in the milk and blend until smooth. Sift together dry ingredients and add to sweet potato mixture.

Turn dough onto a lightly floured surface and knead 6 times. Use a floured rolling pin to roll out dough to ½-inch thickness. Cut out with a 2-inch round cutter. Place biscuits one inch apart on lightly greased baking sheets. Bake at 400 degrees for 15 minutes or until golden. Makes about 1½ dozen.

Ruth Gomez
Toledo, OH

Spiced Fruit

This is always a Christmas favorite with our family because it's a nice change from the usual vegetable side dishes.

29-oz. can sliced peaches
15¼-oz. can apricot halves
³/₄ c. brown sugar, packed
½ c. white vinegar
4 cinnamon sticks
1 T. whole allspice
1 t. whole cloves
20-oz. can pineapple chunks,
    drained

Drain the juice from the peaches and apricots into a large saucepan; add brown sugar, vinegar, cinnamon sticks, allspice and cloves. Bring to a boil and boil for 5 minutes.

Add pineapple chunks, peaches and apricots to the saucepan; simmer until fruit is warm. Remove cinnamon sticks and cloves. Serves 6 to 8.

Elaine Nichols
Mesa, AZ

Christmas Morning Chile Relleno

Serve with fruit salad and sausage links for a spicy Christmas breakfast.

16-oz. pkg. shredded Cheddar
    cheese
16-oz. pkg. shredded Monterey
    Jack cheese
2 4-oz. cans chopped green chiles
4 eggs
1 c. evaporated milk
¼ c. all-purpose flour

Sprinkle cheese and chiles together alternately in a greased 13"x9" baking pan. Whisk together eggs, milk and flour in a medium bowl and pour over cheese mixture. Bake at 350 degrees for 30 minutes. Let cool slightly before serving. Makes 8 to 10 servings.

Angela Leikem
Silverton, OR

Don't forget the cocoa!

A well spent day brings happy sleep.
— Leonardo Da Vinci

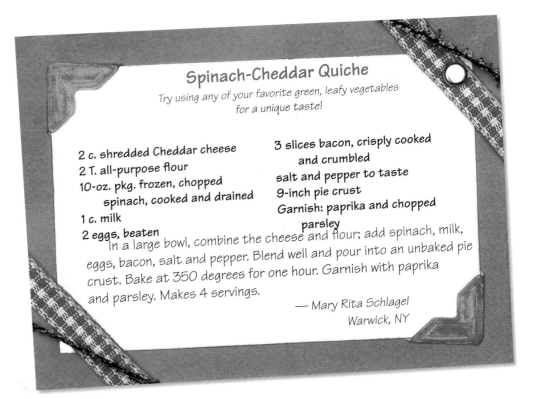

Spinach-Cheddar Quiche

Try using any of your favorite green, leafy vegetables for a unique taste!

2 c. shredded Cheddar cheese
2 T. all-purpose flour
10-oz. pkg. frozen, chopped
   spinach, cooked and drained
1 c. milk
2 eggs, beaten

3 slices bacon, crisply cooked
   and crumbled
salt and pepper to taste
9-inch pie crust
Garnish: paprika and chopped
   parsley

In a large bowl, combine the cheese and flour; add spinach, milk, eggs, bacon, salt and pepper. Blend well and pour into an unbaked pie crust. Bake at 350 degrees for one hour. Garnish with paprika and parsley. Makes 4 servings.

— Mary Rita Schlagel
Warwick, NY

Cranberry-Orange Scones

Cranberry-Orange Scones

During the busy holiday season, my sisters and I always pick one morning to hold our annual "sisters' brunch." We each share special moments, gifts and yummy dishes. This is a favorite!

2 c. all-purpose flour
10 t. sugar, divided
1 T. plus 1 t. orange zest, divided
2 t. baking powder
1/2 t. salt
1/4 t. baking soda
1/3 c. chilled butter
1 c. dried cranberries
1/4 c. plus 1 T. orange juice,
   divided
1/4 c. half-and-half
1 egg
1 T. milk or half-and-half
1/2 c. powdered sugar

Combine flour, 7 teaspoons sugar, one tablespoon orange zest, baking powder, salt and baking soda; cut in butter with a pastry cutter until coarse crumbs form.

In a small bowl, stir cranberries, 1/4 cup orange juice, half-and-half and egg together; add to flour mixture until a soft dough forms. Knead 6 to 8 times on a lightly floured surface; pat into an 8-inch circle. Cut into 8 wedges; separate wedges and place on an ungreased baking sheet. Brush with milk; sprinkle with remaining 3 teaspoons sugar.

Bake at 400 degrees for 12 to 15 minutes; cool slightly. Combine powdered sugar, remaining one tablespoon orange juice and remaining one teaspoon orange zest; drizzle over warm scones. Makes 8.

*Dayna Hansen
Junction City, OR*

Cheddar Cheese Biscuits

Fresh dill and chives make these rolls taste so good.

3 c. all-purpose flour
4$\frac{1}{2}$ t. baking powder
1 T. sugar
1$\frac{1}{2}$ t. dry mustard
1 t. salt
$\frac{1}{4}$ c. unsalted butter, chilled and cut into pieces
$\frac{1}{4}$ c. shortening, chilled and cut into pieces
1 c. plus 2 T. milk
$\frac{1}{4}$ c. chives, chopped
3 T. dill, chopped
2$\frac{1}{2}$ c. sharp Cheddar cheese, grated and divided

Sift together flour, baking powder, sugar, mustard and salt. Cut in butter and shortening until crumbly. Blend together milk, chives and dill, stir into dry ingredients and add in 2 cups cheese.

On a lightly floured surface, knead dough lightly. Roll out dough to $\frac{1}{2}$-inch thickness and cut out using a floured biscuit cutter. Sprinkle biscuit tops with remaining $\frac{1}{2}$ cup cheese, place on lightly greased baking sheets and bake at 450 degrees for 15 minutes. Makes about 1$\frac{1}{2}$ dozen.

Audrey Lett
Newark, DE

Cheese Blintz Casserole

Super with warm jam or fresh berries spooned over each serving.

1$\frac{1}{4}$ c. all-purpose flour
3 T. sugar
1 t. baking powder
$\frac{1}{2}$ c. plus 2 T. butter, softened and divided
$\frac{3}{4}$ c. milk
3 eggs, divided
16-oz. container cottage cheese
1 T. sour cream
$\frac{1}{4}$ t. salt

Combine flour, sugar, baking powder and $\frac{1}{2}$ cup butter in a medium bowl. Stir in milk and 2 eggs; set aside.

Stir together cottage cheese, sour cream, salt, remaining 2 tablespoons butter and remaining egg in a separate bowl; set aside.

Spoon half the flour mixture into a lightly greased 1$\frac{1}{2}$-quart baking dish; top with cottage cheese mixture, then with remaining flour mixture. Bake at 350 degrees for 50 minutes or until puffy and golden. Let cool slightly. Serves 6.

Tori Willis
Champaign, IL

Sunshine Grits

A down-home, delicious comfort food.

3 c. water
1 t. salt
1 c. quick-cooking grits, uncooked
1 c. orange juice
4 eggs, beaten
$\frac{1}{4}$ c. butter
1$\frac{1}{2}$ t. orange zest
2$\frac{1}{4}$ T. brown sugar, packed

Bring water and salt to a boil in a 3-quart saucepan. Pour in grits and cook over medium heat for 3 minutes, stirring constantly; remove from heat.

Stir in orange juice, eggs, butter and orange zest. Spoon into a greased 1$\frac{1}{2}$-quart baking dish; sprinkle with brown sugar.

Bake at 350 degrees for 45 minutes or until a knife inserted in the center comes out clean. Makes 8 servings.

Regina Vining
Warwick, RI

Cooking Ahead to the Holidays

Make it easy on yourself with Vickie & Jo Ann's fix-ahead dishes by freezing them before the holidays begin. The comfort-food casseroles and soups are complemented by the yummy breads and desserts. Prepare some ingredients ahead of time, like slicing veggies and cooking meat, so you can join in the fun instead of spending Christmas in the kitchen!

Turkey and Wild Rice Casserole

Turkey and Wild Rice Casserole

Make this before the holidays and prepare it again with the turkey left after Christmas dinner.

**6.2-oz. pkg. long-grain and
   wild rice mix, uncooked
1/2 lb. ground pork sausage
1 c. sliced mushrooms
1/2 c. celery, sliced
1 T. cornstarch
1 c. milk
1 T. Worcestershire sauce
3 c. cooked turkey, chopped
1 c. sweetened dried cranberries**

Prepare rice mix according to package directions and set aside.

Cook sausage, mushrooms and celery in a large skillet until sausage is browned, stirring to crumble meat. Drain sausage mixture, reserving one tablespoon drippings in skillet. Set sausage mixture aside.

Add cornstarch to drippings in skillet, stirring until smooth. Cook one minute, stirring constantly. Gradually add milk and Worcestershire sauce; cook over medium heat, stirring constantly, until mixture is thickened.

Combine rice, sausage mixture, sauce, turkey and cranberries. Spoon mixture into a lightly greased 11"x7" baking dish.

To Store: Cover and refrigerate up to 2 days. Cover tightly and freeze up to 2 weeks.

To Serve: Thaw in refrigerator. Bake, uncovered, at 375 degrees for 40 to 45 minutes. Makes 6 to 8 servings.

Cheesy Sausage-and-Tomato Manicotti

Cheesy Sausage-and-Tomato Manicotti

Use two 11"x7" baking dishes and take one to a neighbor to enjoy during the busy holidays. What a delicious gift!

8-oz. pkg. manicotti noodles, uncooked
15-oz. can tomato sauce
10-oz. can diced tomatoes and green chiles with garlic, oregano and basil
1 lb. Italian sausage
8-oz. pkg. cream cheese
1 c. ricotta cheese
4 c. shredded mozzarella cheese, divided

Cook pasta according to package directions; rinse with cold water. Drain.

Process tomato sauce and diced tomatoes in a blender 20 seconds or until smooth. Set aside.

Remove casings from sausage and discard. Cook sausage in a large skillet over medium-high heat, stirring until meat crumbles and is no longer pink. Stir in cream cheese, ricotta cheese and 2 cups mozzarella cheese. Spoon into manicotti shells; arrange stuffed shells in a lightly greased 13"x9" baking dish.

Pour tomato mixture over shells; sprinkle with remaining 2 cups mozzarella cheese.

Bake at 350 degrees for 20 minutes or until cheese is melted and bubbly. Let casserole stand 10 minutes before serving. Makes 6 servings.

To Store: Casserole can be assembled, tightly covered and frozen up to one month.

To Serve: Thaw in refrigerator overnight; bake, covered, at 350 degrees for 30 minutes. Uncover and bake 15 more minutes or until cheese is melted and bubbly.

Ground Beef-and-Tomato Manicotti: Substitute one pound lean ground beef for sausage. Stir in ½ teaspoon dried Italian seasoning, one teaspoon salt, one teaspoon pepper and one teaspoon fennel seed. Proceed as directed.

Cheesy Chicken Curry Casserole

Having guests during the holidays will be a breeze with this dish waiting in the freezer.

2 c. cooked chicken, chopped
2 c. cooked broccoli flowerets
10¾-oz. can cream of chicken soup
1 c. sour cream
1 c. shredded Cheddar cheese
¾ c. milk
1 t. curry powder
½ t. black pepper
¼ t. garlic powder
Optional: ⅛ t. red pepper
½ c. fine, dry breadcrumbs
2 T. butter or margarine, melted

Combine first 9 ingredients; add red pepper, if desired. Spoon into a lightly greased 11"x7" baking dish.

Bake at 350 degrees for 30 minutes or until hot and bubbly. Stir together breadcrumbs and melted butter; sprinkle over casserole and bake 10 more minutes. Let stand 5 minutes before serving. Makes 6 servings.

To Store: Freeze unbaked casserole, omitting breadcrumbs and butter, for up to one month.

To Serve: Allow to stand at room temperature one hour. Bake at 350 degrees for one hour and 30 minutes or until hot and bubbly. Stir together breadcrumbs and melted butter; sprinkle over casserole and bake 10 more minutes. Let stand 5 minutes before serving.

Smoky Red Beans and Rice

Country Corn Cakes

When you make these ahead, you won't be standing in the kitchen cooking when the family is ready to eat.

10-oz. pkg. frozen corn, thawed
2 T. onion, finely chopped
2 T. celery, finely chopped
2-oz. jar diced pimiento, drained
1½ c. buttermilk
1 egg, lightly beaten
2 T. butter or margarine, melted
¼ t. salt
1¾ c. self-rising cornmeal
¼ c. vegetable oil, divided

Finely chop ½ cup corn. Combine chopped and unchopped corn, onion and next 6 ingredients in a medium bowl; stir well. Gradually add cornmeal, stirring just until moistened.

Heat 2 tablespoons oil in a large skillet over medium-high heat. Pour ¼ cup batter into skillet for each corn cake, cooking 3 to 4 cakes at a time. Cook 4 to 5 minutes on each side or until golden. Drain cakes on paper towels. Repeat procedure using remaining batter and adding oil to skillet, if necessary. Cool.

To Store: Refrigerate corn cakes in a tightly covered container up to 2 days. Freeze corn cakes in an airtight container up to one month.

To Serve: Place cakes on ungreased baking sheets. Bake at 350 degrees for 10 to 12 minutes or until thoroughly heated. Makes 14.

Smoky Red Beans and Rice

Be sure and put the name of the dish and the date on a label before freezing.

½ lb. dried red beans
6 c. water, divided
¾ c. onion, chopped
½ c. celery, chopped
½ c. green pepper, chopped
2 cloves garlic, minced
2 T. parsley, chopped
1 bay leaf
½ t. salt
½ t. red pepper flakes
½ lb. smoked Polish sausage, cut into ¼-inch pieces
hot cooked rice

Combine dried red beans and 3 cups water in a large saucepan. Bring to a boil; reduce heat and simmer 2 minutes. Remove from heat; cover and let stand one hour. Drain well.

Return beans to saucepan. Add remaining 3 cups water, onion and next 7 ingredients. Bring to a boil; cover, reduce heat and simmer 2 hours or until beans are tender, stirring occasionally. Add sausage and simmer, uncovered, an additional 30 minutes. Remove and discard bay leaf. Cool.

To Store: Refrigerate bean mixture in a tightly covered container up to 3 days. Freeze in an airtight container up to 2 weeks.

To Serve: Thaw in refrigerator. Place bean mixture in a large saucepan. Cook over medium-low heat until thoroughly heated, stirring occasionally. Serve over rice. Makes 8 servings.

Sour Cream-Streusel Pound Cake

A tried-&-true recipe that will become a holiday tradition in your family.

1/2 c. brown sugar, packed
1/4 c. chopped pecans
2 T. butter or margarine, softened
2 T. all-purpose flour
1 t. cinnamon
1 c. butter or margarine, softened
3 c. sugar
6 eggs
3 c. all-purpose flour
1/4 t. baking powder
1/4 t. baking soda
1/4 t. salt
1 c. sour cream
2 t. vanilla extract

Combine first 5 ingredients, stirring well. Set aside.

Beat one cup butter at medium speed with an electric mixer, gradually adding sugar. Add eggs, one at a time, beating well after each addition.

Combine 3 cups flour, baking powder, baking soda and salt; add to butter mixture alternately with sour cream, beginning and ending with flour mixture. Mix just until blended after each addition. Stir in vanilla.

Pour half of batter into a greased and floured 12-cup Bundt® pan. Sprinkle pecan mixture over batter; pour remaining batter over pecan mixture. Bake at 325 degrees for one hour and 15 minutes or until a wooden pick inserted in center comes out clean. Cool in pan 10 minutes; remove from pan and cool completely on a wire rack. Makes one 10" cake.

To Store: Cover and store at room temperature up to 3 days. Cover tightly and freeze up to one month.

To Serve: Thaw at room temperature.

Lemon-Orange Rolls

These are so quick when you use a hot roll mix. Freeze several batches and give as gifts to your hairdresser, mail carrier and newspaper delivery person.

16-oz. pkg. hot roll mix
1/4 c. butter, softened and divided
2/3 c. sugar
2 T. orange zest
1 T. lemon zest
2 c. powdered sugar
1/4 c. orange juice

Prepare hot roll dough according to package directions.

Divide dough into 2 equal portions. Roll one portion of dough into a 12"x8" rectangle on a lightly floured surface. Spread with 2 tablespoons butter.

Stir together sugar and zests; sprinkle half of sugar mixture evenly over butter on dough. Roll up dough, jelly-roll style, starting at a long edge. Repeat procedure with remaining half of dough, 2 tablespoons butter and remaining half of sugar mixture.

Cut each roll into 1/2-inch thick slices and place in lightly greased miniature muffin pans.

Cover and let rise in a warm place (85 degrees), free from drafts, 20 minutes.

Bake at 375 degrees for 8 to 10 minutes or until golden. Remove from pans and place on wire racks.

Stir together powdered sugar and orange juice until smooth; spoon evenly over tops of rolls. Makes 4 dozen.

To Store: Glazed rolls can be baked up to one month ahead and frozen in plastic zipping bags.

To Serve: Thaw at room temperature. Reheat, uncovered, at 350 degrees for 3 to 5 minutes.

Lemon-Orange Rolls

Cookie Exchange

A cookie swap is a fun way for you and your friends to sample an assortment of homemade cookies for the holidays while only baking one kind! Invite your guests to bring a dozen cookies for each person who will be attending. Provide labels for the cookies and take-home tins or boxes so your guests can easily gather their share of the home-baked goodies. In this selection of recipes, we're including a dozen yummy cookies that are perfect for exchanging, as well as a couple of candies for everyone to enjoy during the party.

Vanilla-Dipped Gingersnaps

Vanilla-Dipped Gingersnaps

This is a cookie recipe I make every Christmas for friends & family. These are not only pretty, but they taste delicious.

2¹/₂ c. sugar, divided
1¹/₂ c. oil
2 eggs
¹/₂ c. molasses
4 c. all-purpose flour
4 t. baking soda
1 T. ground ginger
2 t. cinnamon
1 t. salt
2 11-oz. pkgs. white chocolate
    chips
¹/₄ c. shortening

Combine 2 cups sugar and oil in a mixing bowl; mix well. Add eggs, one at a time, beating well after each addition. Stir in molasses.

Combine flour, baking soda, ginger, cinnamon and salt in a separate bowl; gradually blend into molasses mixture. Shape dough into one-inch balls and roll in remaining sugar; place 2 inches apart on ungreased baking sheets. Bake at 350 degrees for 15 to 20 minutes or until cookie springs back when lightly touched. Remove to wire racks to cool.

Melt white chocolate chips and shortening together in a small saucepan over low heat, stirring until smooth. Dip each cookie halfway into mixture; allow excess to drip off. Place cookies on wax paper to harden. Makes about 7 dozen.

Krista Starnes
Beaufort, SC

Jolly Lime Thumbprints

Jolly Lime Thumbprints

Refreshing lime adds just the right amount of flavor to these cookies!

¹/₂ c. butter, softened
¹/₄ c. sugar
1 egg yolk
1¹/₂ t. vanilla extract
1¹/₄ c. all-purpose flour
¹/₄ t. salt

Beat butter, sugar, egg yolk and vanilla together for one to 2 minutes with an electric mixer on medium speed. Reduce speed to low; add flour and salt, blending well.

Shape dough into one-inch balls and place one inch apart on ungreased baking sheets. Make an indentation in the center of each ball using your thumb or the back of a teaspoon. Bake at 350 degrees for 12 to 15 minutes. Remove to a wire rack to cool completely. Spoon filling into centers of cookies. Makes about 2 dozen.

Filling:
¹/₃ c. sugar
2 T. lime juice
1 T. lime zest
1 egg yolk
1 to 2 drops green food coloring

Combine first 4 ingredients in a small saucepan; heat over medium heat until mixture boils and begins to thicken, stirring constantly. Remove from heat; stir in food coloring. Set aside to cool to room temperature.

Heavenly Cookies
Craving chocolate? Try these double-chocolate and candy bar cookies!

1 c. butter, softened
2¹/₂ c. powdered sugar
2 eggs
2 t. vanilla extract
2¹/₂ c. all-purpose flour
1 t. baking soda
1 t. salt
¹/₂ c. white chocolate chips
1¹/₂ c. semi-sweet chocolate chunks
4 1.4-oz. toffee candy bars, crushed
Optional: ¹/₂ c. chopped pecans

Combine butter, powdered sugar, eggs and vanilla; mix well. Add flour, baking soda and salt; mix until well blended. Stir in white chocolate chips, chocolate chunks, candy bar pieces and nuts, if using. Drop by tablespoonfuls onto ungreased baking sheets. Bake at 350 degrees for 12 to 15 minutes or until golden. Makes 2 dozen.

Joy Diomede
Double Oak, TX

Cheerful Chorus of Carolers
Bake these for the church choir to let them know they're appreciated!

³/₄ c. butter, softened
1 c. sugar
¹/₂ t. baking powder
¹/₂ t. salt
1 egg
1¹/₂ t. vanilla extract
2¹/₂ c. all-purpose flour
Garnish: baking cocoa, oval-shaped multi-colored sprinkles, red and desired food coloring, corn syrup

Combine butter and sugar in a large mixing bowl; blend in baking powder and salt. Stir in egg and vanilla; gradually blend in flour. Divide dough in half; shape each half into a 6-inch long roll. Wrap in plastic wrap; refrigerate overnight or until firm.

Cut dough into ¹/₄-inch thick slices, reserving an inch of dough from each roll for decorations. Arrange rounds on ungreased baking sheets; use a drinking straw to make a round hole in each circle for the caroler's mouth. Tint some of the remaining dough with cocoa; press tinted and untinted dough through a garlic press to make the hair. Tint remaining dough to make hats, scarves and earmuffs to decorate carolers as desired. Use sprinkles for eyes and noses.

Bake at 375 degrees for 6 to 8 minutes; cool on wire racks, reshaping mouths if necessary by reopening with a straw. Tint one teaspoon corn syrup with red food coloring and brush on cookies to make rosy cheeks. Makes about 3 dozen.

Chocolate & Vanilla Swirl Cookies
Two colors and flavors that make a great cookie.

¹/₂ c. butter, softened
1 c. sugar
2 t. baking powder
¹/₄ t. salt
1 egg
2 T. milk
1¹/₂ t. vanilla extract
2 c. all-purpose flour
1-oz. sq. unsweetened baking chocolate, melted and cooled

Beat butter, sugar, baking powder and salt until light and fluffy; blend in egg, milk and vanilla. Mix in flour; divide dough in half. Blend melted chocolate into one half; divide both chocolate dough and vanilla dough into 2 equal portions.

Roll out one portion of chocolate dough on a lightly floured surface into a 9"x5" rectangle; set aside. Roll out one portion of vanilla dough into the same size; carefully place vanilla dough on top of chocolate dough, patting down lightly. Starting at one short side, roll dough layers up together. Repeat with remaining 2 portions of dough. Wrap both logs in plastic wrap and refrigerate at least 3 hours.

Cut dough into ¹/₄-inch thick slices and place on greased baking sheets. Bake at 350 degrees for 8 to 10 minutes; cool on wire racks. Makes about 3 dozen.

Sweet Chocolate-Toffee Delights

The creamy filling makes these bars extra special.

4 1-oz. sqs. unsweetened baking
   chocolate
1 c. butter
2 c. sugar
1 t. vanilla extract
4 eggs
1¹/₂ c. all-purpose flour
¹/₂ t. salt
1 c. milk chocolate toffee bits

Melt chocolate and butter together in the top of a double boiler; stir until smooth. Remove from heat; let cool 5 minutes.

Pour into a large mixing bowl; blend in sugar, vanilla and eggs. Add flour and salt; mix well. Pour half the batter into a greased 13"x9" baking pan; spread with filling. Pour remaining batter on top; sprinkle with toffee bits. Bake at 350 degrees for 45 to 50 minutes or until a toothpick inserted in the center comes out clean; cool completely. Cut into bars. Makes about 4 dozen.

Filling:
2 8-oz. pkgs. cream cheese,
   softened
¹/₂ c. sugar
1 egg
1 t. vanilla extract
1 c. milk chocolate toffee bits

Blend first 4 ingredients together; fold in toffee bits.

Chocolate Chip Macaroon Bars

Tuck these in an old-fashioned cookie jar for gift-giving.

¹/₂ c. butter, softened
1 c. plus 2 T. all-purpose flour,
   divided
1¹/₂ c. brown sugar, packed and
   divided
2 eggs
¹/₄ t. salt
1 c. chopped pecans
1¹/₂ c. flaked coconut
1 t. vanilla extract
1 c. chocolate chips

Mix together butter, one cup flour and ¹/₂ cup brown sugar. Pat into the bottom of a 13"x9" greased baking pan. Bake at 325 degrees for 15 minutes.

In a medium bowl, blend together remaining 2 tablespoons flour, remaining one cup brown sugar, eggs, salt, pecans, coconut, vanilla and chocolate chips. Spread mixture onto baked crust. Bake for an additional 25 minutes. Cut into bars when cool. Makes about 4 dozen.

Sheryl Thomas
Potterville, MI

Magic Window Cookies

My kids love to make these!

³/₄ c. shortening
1 c. sugar
2 eggs
1 t. vanilla extract
2¹/₂ c. all-purpose flour
1 t. baking powder
1 t. salt
6 pkgs. hard candy, crushed

Mix together shortening, sugar, eggs and vanilla. Blend in flour, baking powder and salt. Cover and chill at least one hour.

Roll out dough to ¹/₈-inch thickness on a lightly floured cloth-covered board. Cut dough with cookie cutters that have a cutout in the middle or if using regular cookie cutters, cut out center of dough with mini cookie cutters. Place cookies on aluminum foil-covered baking sheets. Place crushed candy in the cookie cutouts, filling cutouts until candy is level with the dough. Bake cookies at 375 degrees for 7 to 9 minutes. Makes 3 or more dozen depending on size of cutouts.

Anne Tufo
Heath, TX

Sweet Chocolate-Toffee Delights

Orange Cookies

My Grandma used to bake these at Christmas. She was a great cook and a very special lady.

1 1/2 c. brown sugar, packed
3/4 c. butter, softened
2 eggs
1 t. vanilla extract
1 1/2 t. orange zest
1/2 c. milk
1 1/2 t. vinegar
3 c. all-purpose flour
1 1/2 t. baking powder
1/2 t. baking soda
1/4 t. salt
Optional: 3/4 c. chopped walnuts

Combine brown sugar, butter, eggs, vanilla and zest, blending after each addition. Set aside. Mix together milk and vinegar; stir to blend and add to brown sugar mixture. Set aside. Combine flour, baking powder, baking soda and salt; blend well and add to brown sugar mixture. Stir in walnuts, if using. Drop by teaspoonfuls onto greased baking sheets. Bake at 350 degrees for 8 to 10 minutes. Spread Orange Frosting on cooled cookies. Makes 3 to 4 dozen.

Orange Frosting:
1 c. powdered sugar
1/3 c. orange juice
1 1/2 t. orange zest

Combine all ingredients; mix well.

DeeAnn Portra
Turtle Lake, ND

Holiday Peppermint Fudge

Merry Spritz-mas Cookies

A cookie press makes these cookies look special.

1 1/2 c. butter, softened
1 c. sugar
1 egg
1 1/2 t. lemon extract
3 1/2 c. all-purpose flour
1 t. baking powder
4 to 5 drops red food coloring
4 to 5 drops green food coloring

Beat butter and sugar until fluffy. Add egg and lemon extract; blend well. Stir in flour and baking powder. Divide dough into 3 equal portions; tint one portion with red food coloring, one portion with green food coloring and leave remaining portion untinted. Roll portions into 1/2-inch wide logs; stack logs with untinted dough in the middle. Cut stacked log into 6-inch portions and gently place one portion into a cookie press; attach desired plate to cookie press. Force dough through press onto ungreased baking sheets. Repeat with remaining portions. Bake at 375 degrees for 6 to 8 minutes; remove to cool on wire racks. Makes about 5 dozen.

Holiday Peppermint Fudge

A quick, easy candy.

4 c. sugar
2 5-oz. cans evaporated milk
1 c. butter
2 c. semi-sweet chocolate chips
7-oz. jar marshmallow creme
1/2 t. peppermint extract
2/3 c. red and white peppermint candies, coarsely broken

Combine sugar, milk and butter in a heavy 4-quart saucepan; bring to a boil over medium-high heat, stirring constantly. Reduce heat to medium; cook and stir for 10 minutes. Remove from heat; add chocolate chips, marshmallow creme and peppermint extract. Stir until chocolate and creme are melted and mixture is smooth; pour into a buttered aluminum foil-lined 13"x9" baking pan. Sprinkle with candies; cover and refrigerate until set.

Cut into squares. Makes 5 to 6 dozen.

Best-Ever Candy Bar Squares

Oats, chocolate, peanut butter, butterscotch and peanuts make this a winning combination.

1 c. brown sugar, packed
2/3 c. butter
1/4 c. corn syrup
1 c. creamy peanut butter, divided
1 t. vanilla extract
3 1/2 c. quick-cooking oats, uncooked
2 c. semi-sweet chocolate chips
1 c. butterscotch chips
1 c. peanuts, chopped and divided

Combine brown sugar, butter and corn syrup in a saucepan; heat over medium heat until sugar dissolves and butter melts. Remove from heat. Stir in 1/4 cup peanut butter and vanilla until smooth; set aside.

Place oats in a large mixing bowl; stir in brown sugar mixture. Line a 13"x9" baking pan with aluminum foil; grease foil. Press oats mixture into the bottom of prepared pan; bake at 375 degrees for 15 to 18 minutes.

Melt chocolate chips and butterscotch chips together over low heat; stir in remaining 3/4 cup peanut butter until smooth. Set aside.

Sprinkle 1/2 cup peanuts over crust; slowly pour melted chocolate mixture on top, spreading evenly. Sprinkle with remaining 1/2 cup peanuts; cool until firm. Cut into squares; cover and refrigerate until ready to serve. Makes 5 dozen.

Yummy Cappuccino Bites

Just the right amount of coffee flavor in these cookies!

1/3 c. butter, softened
1 c. brown sugar, packed
2/3 c. baking cocoa
1 T. instant coffee granules
1 t. baking soda
1 t. cinnamon
2 egg whites
1/3 c. vanilla yogurt
1 1/2 c. all-purpose flour
1/3 c. sugar

Combine butter and brown sugar. Stir in cocoa, coffee granules, baking soda and cinnamon. Mix in egg whites and yogurt; blend in flour. Place sugar in a small bowl; drop dough by heaping teaspoonfuls into sugar. Roll into one-inch balls and place 2 inches apart on ungreased baking sheets. Bake at 350 degrees for 8 to 10 minutes; cool on wire racks. Makes about 2 1/2 dozen.

Prize-Winning Peanut Butter Cups

A yummy treat!

60 1-inch miniature paper baking cups
9 1-oz. sqs. white baking chocolate, chopped
1 1/2 c. creamy peanut butter, divided
8 1-oz. sqs. semi-sweet baking chocolate, chopped
1/2 c. peanuts, chopped

Place baking cups in a jelly-roll pan; set aside.

Melt white chocolate and 3/4 cup peanut butter in a heavy saucepan over low heat, stirring constantly; spoon into baking cups. Refrigerate for 10 minutes.

Melt semi-sweet chocolate and remaining 3/4 cup peanut butter in a heavy saucepan over low heat, stirring constantly; spoon on top of white chocolate mixture. Sprinkle with chopped peanuts; refrigerate overnight. Makes 5 dozen.

Best-Ever Candy Bar Squares

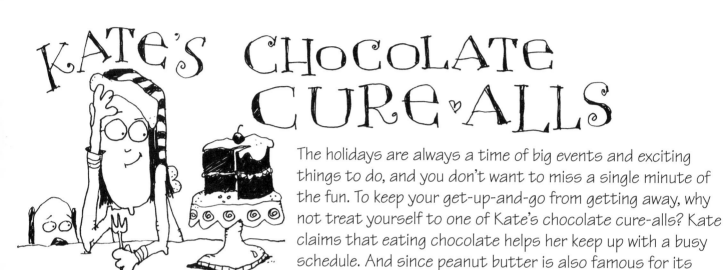

KATE'S CHOCOLATE CURE♥ALLS

The holidays are always a time of big events and exciting things to do, and you don't want to miss a single minute of the fun. To keep your get-up-and-go from getting away, why not treat yourself to one of Kate's chocolate cure-alls? Kate claims that eating chocolate helps her keep up with a busy schedule. And since peanut butter is also famous for its energy-boosting abilities, she says you ought to start with a rich and fudgy Buckeye Brownie. Feel like sharing this treasure trove of vitality enhancers? Make extras for gifts!

Buckeye Brownies

Chocolate and peanut butter...tastes just like buckeye candies.

19½-oz. pkg. brownie mix
2 c. powdered sugar
½ c. plus 6 T. butter, softened and
    divided
1 c. creamy peanut butter
6-oz. pkg. semi-sweet chocolate
    chips

Prepare and bake brownie mix in a greased 13"x9" baking pan according to package directions. Let cool.

Mix together powdered sugar, ½ cup butter and peanut butter; spread over cooled brownies. Chill for one hour.

Melt together chocolate chips and remaining 6 tablespoons butter in a saucepan over low heat, stirring occasionally. Spread over brownies. Let cool; cut into squares. Makes 2 to 3 dozen.

Heather Prentice
Mars, PA

Buckeye Brownies

Pan O' Fudge

You will need to make more than one pan of this delicious fudge!

4¹/₂ c. sugar
12-oz. can evaporated milk
1¹/₂ c. butter
12-oz. pkg. semi-sweet chocolate
    chips
1 t. vanilla extract
¹/₂ c. chopped nuts

Combine sugar and milk in saucepan; boil for 6 minutes. Remove from heat. Add butter, chocolate chips and vanilla. Beat 10 minutes with mixer; stir in nuts. Pour into buttered 8"x8" pan. Makes about 1 pound.

Sue Utley
Papillion, NE

White Hot Chocolate

This hot chocolate will warm you head-to-toe.

12-oz. bar white chocolate, finely
    chopped
6 c. milk
2 c. whipping cream
1 t. vanilla extract
Garnish: milk chocolate shavings

Place white chocolate in a medium bowl; set aside.
Combine milk and cream in a saucepan; heat over medium heat until bubbles begin to form around edges, about 4 minutes. Do not boil. Pour over white chocolate. When chocolate begins to melt, gently stir to combine. Whisk in vanilla. Pour into mugs. Sprinkle with chocolate shavings and serve immediately. Makes 8 cups.

Dawn Brown
Vandenberg AFB, CA

Triple Chocolate Cake

A chocolate lover's delight.

18¹/₄-oz. pkg. devil's food cake mix
4¹/₂-oz. pkg. instant chocolate
    pudding mix
1³/₄ c. milk
12-oz. pkg. semi-sweet chocolate
    chips
2 eggs
Garnish: powdered sugar

Combine cake mix, pudding mix, milk, chocolate chips and eggs in a large bowl. Mix by hand until well blended, about 2 minutes. Pour batter into a greased and floured Bundt® pan. Bake at 350 degrees for 50 to 55 minutes or until cake springs back when touched. Do not overbake. Turn out onto a serving plate; sift powdered sugar on top before serving. Serves 10 to 12.

Jane Harm
Neenah, WI

Chocolate Chip Cheesecake Squares

As good as its name!

2 18-oz. tubes refrigerated
    chocolate chip cookie dough
non-stick vegetable spray
3 3-oz. pkgs. cream cheese,
    softened
3 eggs
1 t. vanilla extract

Press one tube of cookie dough into the bottom of a 13"x9" baking pan that has been sprayed with non-stick vegetable spray. Beat cream cheese, eggs and vanilla in a mixing bowl until smooth. Pour over cookie dough; crumble remaining cookie dough over top. Bake at 350 degrees for 30 minutes. Chill before serving. Makes 15 servings.

Jan Brown
Greenwood, AR

Hot Cocoa Cake

Hot Cocoa Cake

The warmth and coziness of hot chocolate on a plate!

$^1/_2$ c. shortening
$^3/_4$ c. sugar
2 eggs
$1^1/_2$ c. all-purpose flour
2 t. baking powder
$^3/_4$ t. salt
$^2/_3$ c. milk
4 T. or 1 env. instant hot cocoa
Optional: powdered sugar and
    chopped nuts

Beat shortening, sugar and eggs until mixture is fluffy. Add flour, baking powder and salt alternately with milk, beating well after each addition. Spoon half of batter into a well-greased 6-cup Bundt® pan. Sprinkle envelope of hot cocoa mix evenly over the batter. Top with the rest of the batter and spread evenly in pan.

Bake at 350 degrees for 35 minutes or until a toothpick comes out clean. Let stand 5 minutes and turn out onto serving plate. Delicious served warm as a coffee cake or let cool and dust with a little powdered sugar. If desired, add chopped nuts of any kind in the layer with the hot cocoa mix. Serves 10 to 12.

Chocolate Silk Pie

Cut generous slices of this pie...everyone will love it!

1 c. sugar
$^1/_2$ c. baking cocoa
$^1/_2$ c. all-purpose flour
$^1/_8$ t. salt
2 c. milk
3 egg yolks
4 T. butter
1 t. vanilla extract
9-inch graham cracker crust
8-oz. container frozen whipped
    topping, thawed
$^1/_2$ c. chocolate chips
Garnish: fresh mint leaves

Combine sugar, cocoa, flour and salt in a saucepan over medium heat. Slowly pour in milk, stirring constantly. Stir in egg yolks, stirring well for 5 to 6 minutes. Remove saucepan from heat; stir in butter and vanilla. Pour mixture into crust. Refrigerate for 8 hours.

Top pie with whipped topping and sprinkle with chocolate chips. Garnish with fresh mint leaves. Serves 6 to 8.

Jamie Moffatt
French Lick, IN

Holly's Brownie Blast!

Serve with an explosion of whipped cream or chocolate chip ice cream!

$^1/_2$ c. butter, softened
1 c. sugar
16-oz. can chocolate syrup
4 eggs
1 c. all-purpose flour
Optional: 1 c. chopped nuts

Combine butter and sugar; blend in syrup, eggs and flour. Pour into a greased 13"x9" baking pan; bake at 350 degrees for 25 minutes. Frost while still warm and garnish with nuts, if desired. Makes 24 servings.

Frosting:
$^1/_2$ c. butter
$1^1/_2$ c. sugar
$^1/_3$ c. evaporated milk
$^1/_2$ c. semi-sweet chocolate chips
1 t. vanilla extract
$^1/_8$ t. salt

Combine butter, sugar and milk in a heavy saucepan; bring to a boil for one minute. Remove from heat; stir in chocolate chips, vanilla and salt until mixture is smooth.

Cheryl Duell
Marietta, OH

Chocolate Snappers

These won't stay in the cookie jar for long!

3/4 c. shortening
1 c. sugar
1 egg
1/4 c. corn syrup
2 oz. unsweetened baking
    chocolate, melted
1 3/4 c. all-purpose flour
2 t. baking soda
1 t. cinnamon
1/4 t. salt
additional sugar

Combine shortening and one cup sugar; add egg. Blend in corn syrup and chocolate; add flour, baking soda, cinnamon and salt, mixing well. Shape dough by teaspoonfuls into walnut-size balls; roll in sugar. Place on ungreased baking sheets and bake at 350 degrees for 10 to 12 minutes. Makes about 3 dozen.

Debbi Baker
Green Springs, OH

Favorite Chocolate Pie

This pie is delicious…so quick & easy to make, yet so elegant.

3.4-oz. pkg. cook and serve
    chocolate pudding mix
2 c. whipping cream, divided
1 c. milk
1/2 c. chocolate chips
9-inch chocolate cookie crust
Garnish: chocolate shavings

Mix together pudding mix, one cup whipping cream, milk and chocolate chips in a saucepan; cook over medium heat, stirring until thickened. Cool and pour into crust. Chill until set.

Whip remaining one cup whipping cream until stiff peaks form; spread over pie. Sprinkle with chocolate shavings. Keep refrigerated. Makes 6 to 8 servings.

Tanya Duke
Bethany, OK

Fantasy Fudge Cookies

Buttermilk and molasses give these cookies a great flavor.

2 c. all-purpose flour
1/2 c. baking cocoa
1/2 t. baking soda
1/4 t. salt
1/4 c. shortening
1/2 c. sugar
1 egg
1/2 c. buttermilk
1/2 c. molasses
1 t. vanilla extract
Optional: 3/4 c. chopped walnuts

Combine flour, cocoa, baking soda and salt; set aside.

Beat shortening and sugar in a large mixing bowl; beat in egg, buttermilk and molasses. Stir in vanilla; gradually blend in flour mixture. Fold in walnuts, if desired. Drop by tablespoonfuls 1 1/2 inches apart onto lightly greased baking sheets. Bake at 350 degrees for 12 to 15 minutes or until firm to the touch. Makes about 3 dozen.

Jen Vollmer
Bismarck, ND

Vickie's Chocolate Fondue

Vickie's Chocolate Fondue

Delicious dipping for squares of pound cake, mandarin oranges, cherries and strawberries!

24-oz. pkg. semi-sweet chocolate
    chips
1 pt. whipping cream
6 T. corn syrup
6 T. orange extract

Melt chocolate chips in the top of a double boiler; add remaining ingredients and stir to blend. When fondue is warm, spoon into a fondue pot or small slow cooker on low heat to keep sauce warm. Makes 2 1/2 cups.

Vickie

A Club Christmas

When it's time to share a cup of Christmas cheer, be sure to remember your book club, bowling team or knitting guild. These people brighten your life with their humor and friendship, so why not make a real event of the group's holiday get-together? This array of appetizers, snacks and beverages offers something tasty for every appetite. There's even a cheesecake that will satisfy the chocolate cravings of one and all. The menu is planned…now all you have to do is tell your garden society or bunko buddies that this year, the party's at your place!

Not-Your-Usual Party Mix

A tasty munchie no one can resist.

15.6-oz. pkg. crispy rice cereal
    squares
10-oz. pkg. oyster crackers
9.5-oz. pkg. mini cheese-filled
    sandwich crackers
6-oz. pkg. fish-shaped
    crackers
16-oz. pkg. mini pretzel twists
16-oz. pkg. peanuts
12-oz. bottle butter-flavored
    popcorn oil
1-oz. pkg. ranch salad
    dressing mix

Combine cereal, crackers, pretzels and peanuts in a large bowl. Combine oil and salad dressing mix in a small bowl; toss with cracker mixture until evenly coated. Store in an airtight container. Makes 20 servings.

Samantha Starks
Madison, WI

Not-Your-Usual Party Mix

Ham-Cream Cheese Croissants

I like to top these with sour cream and salsa.

1½ c. cooked ham, cubed
8-oz. pkg. cream cheese, softened
12-oz. tube refrigerated croissants

In a medium mixing bowl, combine ham and cream cheese. Unroll and separate croissants; place a dollop of ham mixture on each croissant. Roll up and place on an ungreased baking sheet. Bake, uncovered, at 425 degrees for 15 to 18 minutes. Makes 8 servings.

Donna Vogel
The Colony, TX

Victorian Blackberry Punch

A pretty, rich color and delicious berry flavor.

1½ c. sugar
3 c. water
5 c. ice water
3 c. strongly brewed tea, cooled
2 c. grape juice
1 c. pineapple juice
1 c. blackberry juice
1 c. raspberry juice
juice of 6 lemons
juice of 4 oranges
ice mold
Garnish: lemon and orange slices

Dissolve sugar in 3 cups water in a saucepan. Boil for 5 minutes to make a sugar syrup. Cool.

Combine ice water, tea, sugar syrup and fruit juices in a large container. Pour over ice mold into a punch bowl. Garnish with lemon and orange slices. You may want to try this sometime with cranberry juice instead of blackberry juice. Makes 20 cups.

Herb-Marinated Shrimp

Herb-Marinated Shrimp

You will need to make this appetizer a day ahead to allow the great flavors to blend.

3 qts. water
1 lemon, sliced
4 lbs. large shrimp, unpeeled
2 c. vegetable oil
¼ c. hot pepper sauce
1 T. minced garlic
1 T. olive oil
1½ t. salt
1½ t. seafood seasoning
1½ t. dried basil
1½ t. dried oregano
1½ t. dried thyme
1½ t. parsley, minced

Bring water and lemon to a boil; add shrimp and cook 3 to 5 minutes or until shrimp turn pink. Drain well; rinse with cold water. Chill. Peel and devein shrimp. Place shrimp in a large heavy-duty plastic zipping bag.

Combine vegetable oil and remaining 9 ingredients; stir well and pour over shrimp. Seal bag; marinate in refrigerator 8 hours. Drain before serving. Makes about 18 appetizer servings.

Herb-Marinated Cheese

Yummy with sourdough bread. Make this one to four days before serving.

4 to 6 oz. sharp Cheddar cheese,
   cubed
4 to 6 oz. Provolone cheese, cubed
1/2 c. olive oil
1/4 c. herbal vinegar
3 to 4 cloves garlic, pressed
1 T. parsley, chopped
1/2 t. peppercorns
1/4 t. fennel seed
1 bay leaf

Combine all ingredients in a bowl with a tight-fitting lid; refrigerate and marinate for one to 4 days, stirring and mixing each day.

Remove cheese from the bowl with a slotted spoon and serve with toothpicks.

Lynne Tharan
New Bethlehem, PA

Stuffed Strawberries

Hot Seafood & Artichoke Dip

When company is expected, use a can of crabmeat and a can of shrimp; then double the amount of both the cream cheese and artichokes for an appetizer large enough to feed 'em all.

8-oz. pkg. cream cheese, softened
1 c. sour cream
1.4-oz. pkg. vegetable soup mix
6-oz. can crabmeat or shrimp,
   drained
6-oz. jar marinated artichoke
   hearts, drained and chopped
1/2 c. red pepper, chopped
Optional: 1/2 t. hot pepper sauce

Combine all ingredients and spread in a 13"x9" baking pan. Bake for 25 minutes at 375 degrees. Makes 4 cups.

Joely Flegler
Edmond, OK

Roasted Olives

A sure hit at your next party!

3 c. assorted whole olives
1/4 c. olive oil
4 cloves garlic, thinly sliced
2 T. rosemary, chopped
1 T. lemon zest
1/2 t. pepper
1/2 t. fennel seed, crushed
1/4 t. red pepper flakes

Combine all ingredients in a large bowl. Let stand at room temperature at least 15 minutes or up to several hours to allow flavors to blend.

Place olives in a single layer on an aluminum foil-lined pan. Roast at 425 degrees for 10 to 12 minutes, stirring occasionally. Serve warm or let cool to room temperature. Makes 3 cups.

Stuffed Strawberries

Try using pecans in place of the walnuts for added variety.

20 strawberries, hulled and divided
8-oz. pkg. cream cheese, softened
1/4 c. walnuts, finely chopped
1 T. powdered sugar

Dice 2 strawberries; set aside. Cut a thin layer from the stem end of the remaining strawberries, forming a base. Starting at opposite end of strawberry, slice into 4 wedges, being careful not to slice through the base; set aside.

Beat remaining ingredients together until fluffy; fold in diced strawberries. Spoon 1 1/2 tablespoonfuls into the center of each strawberry. Refrigerate until ready to serve. Makes 18.

Barbara Parham Hyde
Manchester, TN

Brown Sugar Pecans

Seems I am forever making these throughout the holiday season. My family eats them before they're even cooled!

16-oz. pkg. pecan halves
1/2 c. butter
3/4 c. brown sugar, packed
2 t. vanilla extract
1/4 t. salt

Arrange pecan halves in an aluminum foil-lined 13"x9" baking pan; set aside.

Melt butter in a saucepan over medium heat; add brown sugar, vanilla and salt. Stir one minute; remove from heat. Continue stirring until sugar dissolves; pour over pecans, stirring to coat. Bake at 325 degrees for 25 to 35 minutes; stir every 10 to 15 minutes. Remove from oven; spread on wax paper to cool. Store in an airtight container. Makes 12 servings.

Nancy Wise
Little Rock, AR

The Governor's Hot Buttered Coffee

Perfect for a dessert party!

1/4 c. sweet, unsalted butter
2 c. brown sugar, packed
1/4 t. cinnamon
1/4 t. nutmeg
1/4 t. allspice
1/4 t. ground cloves
Optional: 1 oz. dark rum
2 T. whipping cream
freshly brewed coffee, strong and very hot
Garnish: whipped cream

Combine butter and sugar and blend in spices. Refrigerate in a jar until ready to use.

To serve, place a scant tablespoon of the spice mixture in a 10-ounce clear glass, heat-proof mug. Add rum, if desired and whipping cream. Fill each mug with coffee. Garnish with a dollop of whipped cream. Makes 20 servings.

Governor's Inn
Ludlow, VT

Chocolate-Cappuccino Cheesecake

This makes an absolutely delicious cheesecake.

1 1/2 c. pecans, finely chopped
1 1/2 c. chocolate wafer cookies, crushed
1/3 c. butter, melted
2 c. chocolate chips, melted and divided
2 8-oz. pkgs. cream cheese, softened
1 c. brown sugar, packed
4 eggs
1 c. sour cream
1/3 c. cold coffee
2 t. vanilla extract
1/2 c. chocolate chips
1/3 c. whipping cream
2 T. powdered sugar

Mix pecans, cookies and butter together; press into the bottom of a greased 9" springform pan. Bake at 350 degrees for 8 minutes; cool in pan for 10 minutes. Drizzle crust with 1/2 cup melted chocolate; chill for 40 minutes.

Beat cream cheese with an electric mixer until creamy. Gradually add brown sugar, beating well. Add eggs, one at a time, beating after each addition. Add remaining 1 1/2 cups melted chocolate, sour cream, coffee and vanilla; beat until smooth. Pour into pan; bake at 325 degrees for one hour and 5 minutes (center will not be completely set). Turn oven off and partially open oven door; leave cake in oven one hour. Cool completely. Cover and chill 8 hours.

Remove sides of pan. Heat 1/2 cup chocolate chips and whipping cream over low heat, stirring constantly. Stir in powdered sugar until smooth. Drizzle topping over cake. Makes 12 servings.

Sandy Stacy
Medway, OH

Chocolate-Cappuccino Cheesecake

Glass Candy
(also shown on page 11)
2 c. sugar
1 c. water
$^1/_4$ t. cream of tartar
1 T. extract or 1 t. flavored oil
(lemon and orange extracts;
cinnamon and spearmint oils)
liquid food coloring
powdered sugar

Butter the sides of a large saucepan. Combine sugar, water and cream of tartar in pan. Stirring constantly, cook over medium-low heat until sugar dissolves. Using a pastry brush dipped in hot water, wash down any sugar crystals on sides of pan. Attach a candy thermometer to pan, making sure thermometer does not touch bottom of pan. Increase heat to medium and bring to a boil.

Cook, without stirring, until mixture reaches hard-crack stage (approximately 300 to 310 degrees). Test about $^1/_2$ teaspoon mixture in ice water. Mixture will form brittle threads in ice water and will remain brittle when removed from the water. Remove from heat and stir in desired extract or oil and a few drops of food coloring. Pour mixture onto a lightly greased baking sheet. Cool completely.

Break candy into pieces. Roll pieces in powdered sugar, shaking off excess sugar. Store in an airtight container. Makes about one pound.

TIP: We used the following food colorings and flavors for our candies: orange with orange extract, yellow with lemon extract, red with cinnamon oil and green with spearmint oil.

Stencils
(also shown on pages 28-33)
• clear quilt template plastic
• fine-point permanent pen
• craft knife and cutting mat
• spray adhesive
• plastic palette knife
• Snow-Tex™ textural medium

Making your own stencils is easy, thanks to template plastic. Enlarge or reduce the patterns on page 137 as needed or use them as they are. Trace the patterns onto the plastic and carefully cut them out with the craft knife.

To help your stencils stay in place, work in a well-ventilated area and spray each stencil back with adhesive. Pat the stencil on a large felt scrap to remove excess adhesive; allow the adhesive to dry (the felt fibers left on the stencil will keep it from being too sticky). Press the stencil firmly in place on your project. Be sure to include small detail pieces that have been cut away. (If some of the adhesive stays on the felt, you can use embroidery or manicure scissors to snip it away.)

Using the palette knife, work the Snow-Tex™ back and forth over the stencil. Scrape away the excess Snow-Tex with the knife.

Touch up the design and scrape again if needed. Slowly peel up the stencil. It's okay if you stray outside the lines…clean up is easy with a clothing shaver once the Snow-Tex dries.

Window Stencils
(also shown on page 29)
Save the inner cut-outs from your stencils and use them to stencil designs on your windows with spray snow (patterns are on page 137). Hold the cut-outs in place with removable double-sided tape while stenciling.

Advent Calendar

(also shown on page 33)
- $^3/_8$ yd red felt
- $^1/_2$ yd white felt
- fabric glue
- white rickrack
- Stencil supplies (page 110)
- 1"-tall number stencils (We cut ours from a plastic stencil set.)
- white embroidery floss
- white sequins
- silver jingle bells

Make the Christmas countdown extra-exciting…tuck tiny treasures inside the pockets of this calendar for loved ones to find as they await the big day. Refer to Stencils (page 110) before you begin.

1. Cut five $2^1/_2$"x$12^1/_2$" strips and one $12^1/_2$"x$22^1/_2$" calendar piece (round one end for the top) from red felt. Add 1" all around and cut a white felt calendar piece.
2. For the pockets, start at the bottom end of the red calendar piece and pin the strips, $^1/_2$" apart, to the felt.
3. Sew the calendar pieces together. Sew along the bottom edge of each pocket strip; then, sew down the calendar, dividing the strips into 5 pockets each. Glue rickrack along the edges of the red felt.

4. Stencil the sleigh and snowflake patterns (page 137) and the numbers onto the calendar. Add stitched floss-and-sequin snowflakes. For December 25, glue a bell with a rickrack hanger to the pocket.
5. Sew bells to the calendar, catching the ends of a felt and rickrack hanger in the stitching.

Game Board

(also shown on page 35)
- $^3/_8$ yd brown felt
- $^3/_8$ yd cream felt
- clear nylon thread
- spray adhesive
- $^1/_2$ yd green felt
- tracing paper
- green faux leather
- three $^7/_8$" dia. buttons
- $^1/_8$" dia. hole punch

This clever roll-up game board has checkers on one side and backgammon on the other. Use spray adhesive in a well-ventilated area.

Checkerboard

1. Cut a 13" brown felt square and thirty-two $1^5/_8$" cream felt squares.
2. Zigzag the cream squares onto the brown square in a checkerboard pattern.
3. Adhere the brown square to one side of a $15^1/_2$" green felt square.

Backgammon Board

1. Cut a 12"x$13^1/_2$" brown felt piece and 12 each cream and green felt triangles (pattern on page 144).
2. Alternating colors, sew the triangles along the long edges of the brown piece.
3. Adhere the brown piece to the remaining side of the green felt square.

Band

Round the corners of a 2"x$8^1/_2$" faux leather strip. Sew a button to one end. For the buttonhole, punch two holes, $^7/_8$" apart, in the other end and cut a slit between the holes. Roll the game board and fasten the band around it.

Tip: If you don't have checkers, two different colors of buttons are fun alternatives.

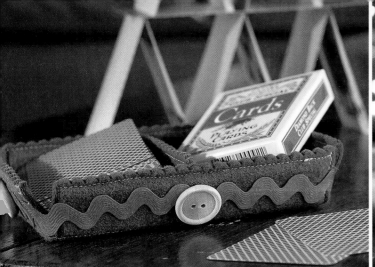

Playing Card Tray

(also shown on page 36)

- mat board
- green felt
- spray adhesive
- scallop-edged scissors
- craft glue
- red rickrack
- clothespins
- buttons

1. For a standard-size card deck tray, cut and arrange mat board pieces on a 9"x10" felt piece as shown in Fig. 1. Working in a well-ventilated area and leaving ¼" between pieces, use spray adhesive to glue the mat board pieces in place.

Fig. 1

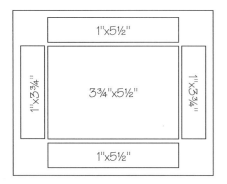

	1"x5½"	
1"x3¾"	3¾"x5½"	1"x3¾"
	1"x5½"	

2. Adhere a second felt piece to the other side of the mat board. Machine sew along the creases between the mat board pieces and around the outer edges close to the mat board. Cut away the excess felt and scallop the edges.
3. Fold the tray sides up and glue rickrack around the outside. Secure with clothespins until the glue dries. Add a button to each side.
4. For the divider, cut a 1"x5" mat board piece and a 3"x5" felt piece. Spray the felt with adhesive and fold it in half over the mat board. Cut the ends away at an angle to fit the tray. Sew along the top edge close to the mat board and scallop the edge. Glue the divider in place.

Santa's Snack Mix

(also shown on page 37)
As far back as I can remember, we've enjoyed this crunchy snack mix…it just wouldn't be Christmas without it.

2 c. crispy corn cereal
2 c. crispy wheat cereal
2 c. crispy rice cereal
2 c. doughnut-shaped
    oat cereal
1 c. pretzel sticks
1 c. halved pecans
6 T. butter, melted
3½ T. Worcestershire sauce
1½ t. seasoned salt
¾ t. garlic powder
½ t. onion powder

In a gallon plastic zipping bag, mix together cereals, pretzels and pecans. To melted butter, add Worcestershire sauce and seasonings; stir to mix. Pour in plastic zipping bag, secure bag and shake to coat. Spoon mix onto a baking sheet and bake at 250 degrees for one hour, stirring every 15 minutes. Cool and store in an airtight container. Makes 10 cups.

Laurie Michael
Colorado Springs, CO

Tabletop Tree Stand

(also shown on page 39)
- black acrylic paint
- paintbrushes
- 2" tallx12½" dia. papier-mâché box without lid
- extra-strength glue
- 12½" dia. metal dog bowl with rubber base
- drill with hole saw or hammer, awl and metal snips
- 9½" length of 1½" dia. PVC pipe
- brown tape
- hot glue gun
- plaster of paris
- dog biscuits or toy dog bones

Spotty will have visions of dog bones dancing in his head when he sees this tempting tree stand. Use with a tabletop tree with a 1¼" dia. trunk.

1. Paint the box. Glue the bowl to the bottom of the box. Make a hole in the bottom of the bowl and box for the pipe to fit through.
2. Wrap the pipe with tape and insert it in the hole. Seal around the pipe inside the bowl with hot glue.
3. Follow manufacturer's instructions to fill the bowl with plaster of paris. Allow the plaster to cure. Pile dog bones on top of the plaster.

Spotty

(also shown on page 38)
- tracing paper
- gray wool felt
- plaid fabric
- armature wire
- wire cutters
- polyester fiberfill
- ³⁄₈" dia. black shank buttons
- black and pink felt scraps
- brown embroidery floss
- ³⁄₄" dia. brown buttons
- alphabet stamps
- black StazOn® ink pad
- metal dog bone tag
- jump ring
- small red collar

This playful watchdog will gladly stand guard over the gifts around the tree. Match right sides and use a ¼" seam allowance.

1. Use the patterns on pages 139-142 and cut these pieces from gray felt: 2 heads (1 in reverse), 2 bodies (1 in reverse), 3 ears, 4 front legs (2 in reverse), 4 back legs (2 in reverse) and 2 tails (1 in reverse). Cut 1 ear from plaid fabric.
2. Leaving openings for turning and openings in the body for attaching the head and tail, sew the parts together in pairs (pair one gray ear with the plaid ear). Turn right side out.

3. Bending the wire into a "J," insert one end of a 13" wire length into the tail. Stuff the head, body and tail. Turn the raw edges of the body ¼" to the wrong side and sew the head and tail to the body. Sew the black buttons to the head for the eyes and add a black felt nose and pink felt tongue.
4. For each ear, curl one end of a 14½" wire length into a "P." Slide this end into the ear and lightly stuff the ear. Cut a small hole in the head and slide the other wire end into the head. Turn the raw edges ¼" to the wrong side and *Whipstitch* (page 129) each ear to the head. Sew plaid spots on the dog.
5. Stuff the legs and sew the openings closed. Work brown *Straight Stitches* at the end of each paw to add toes. Adding a brown button on the outside of each, sew the legs to the body.
6. Stamp a name on the tag. Use the jump ring to attach the tag to the collar and fasten it around the dog's neck.

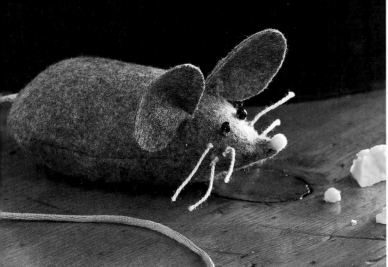

Mouse

(also shown on page 40)
- tracing paper
- gray wool felt
- polyester fiberfill
- knotted tan cord length for
  the tail
- fabric glue
- $1/4$" dia. pink pom-pom
- black E beads
- tan pearl cotton

While Kitty isn't looking, this little mouse sneaks out for a snack. Match right sides and use a $1/4$" seam allowance.

1. Use the patterns on page 140 and cut 2 bodies and 2 ears from felt. Leaving an opening at the back for stuffing, sew the bodies together. Turn right side out, stuff and sew the opening closed, catching the tail.
2. Glue the pom-pom to the body for the nose. Sew the beads in place for the eyes. Knotting close to the face, sew pearl cotton whiskers to the face.
3. Pinch the bottom of the ears to pleat and sew them to the body.

Kitty

(also shown on page 38)
- tracing paper
- tan wool fabric
- polyester fiberfill
- blush or chalk and applicator
- $3/8$" dia. black shank buttons
- pink and brown embroidery floss
- gold pearl cotton
- $3/4$" dia. silver buttons

Kitty is poised to pounce at the first sight of presents. Match right sides and use a $1/4$" seam allowance.

1. Use the patterns on pages 139-141 and cut these pieces from fabric: 2 heads, 2 bodies (1 in reverse), 4 ears, 4 front legs (2 in reverse), 4 back legs (2 in reverse) and 2 tails (1 in reverse).
2. Excluding the head and body and leaving openings for turning, sew the parts together in pairs. Turn right side out.
3. Stuff the tail and front legs and pin them in place between the body pieces. Leaving an opening for turning, sew the body together. Turn right side out, stuff and sew the opening closed.

4. Stuff the ears and sew $3/8$" from the edges of each to form the inner ear. Sew about 1" up the center of the inner ear to make a slight fold. Blush the inner ear. Pin the ears in place between the head pieces. Leaving an opening for turning, sew the head together. Turn right side out, stuff and sew the opening closed.
5. For the eyes, sew the black buttons to the head through all layers. Add a pink *Satin Stitch* (page 129) nose and brown *Chain Stitch* (page 128) mouth. Knotting close to the face, sew pearl cotton whiskers to the face. Sew the head to the body.
6. Stuff the back legs and sew the openings closed. Work brown *Straight Stitches* at the end of each paw to add toes. Adding a silver button on the outside of each, sew the legs to the body.

Snowflake Package Embellishment
(also shown on page 43)
- bleach pen
- snowflake rubber stamp
- blue and light green cardstock
- foam brush
- craft glue
- mica flakes
- ribbon
- gift box
- green scrapbook paper
- deckle-edged scissors
- adhesive foam dots

1. Using the bleach pen as ink, stamp a snowflake on blue cardstock and cut out. Cut a slightly larger light green cardstock piece.
2. Brush glue on the light green piece; adhere the snowflake to the center and sprinkle mica flakes along the edges. Allow to dry and shake off the excess.
3. Cut ribbon long enough to wrap around the box and overlap at the back. Thread the ribbon through slits cut near the short ends of a scrapbook paper rectangle. Cut a slightly larger light green cardstock rectangle with the deckle-edged scissors.
4. Repeat step 2 to glue and glitter the rectangles. Attach the snowflake with foam dots.

5. Wrap a second ribbon length around the box and glue the ends at the back. Glue the rectangles to the box and the first ribbon ends to the back.

XOXO Package Embellishment
(also shown on page 43)
- glue dots
- white gift box
- glitter in assorted colors
- $1/4$"w and $1^3/4$"w ribbon
- $1/4$" dia. hole punch
- metal XOXO tag
- craft glue
- tracing paper
- green cardstock
- spray adhesive
- adhesive foam dot

Apply glue dots to the box, sprinkle with glitter and shake off the excess. Thread the $1/4$" ribbon through holes punched in the tag. Layer and wrap the ribbons around the box. Overlap and glue the ends. Use the pattern on page 150 and cut a cardstock tree. Working in a well-ventilated area, spray the tree with adhesive. Sprinkle glitter on the tree, allow to dry and shake off the excess. Adhere the tree to the box with the foam dot.

Snowflake Ornament
(also shown on page 42)
- white cardstock
- tracing paper
- craft knife and cutting mat
- craft glue
- foam brush
- fine crystal glitter
- $1/4$"w sheer white ribbon

Fold two 6" cardstock squares in half. Use the pattern on page 150 and cut a snowflake from each folded square. Glue the folded centers together, back to back. Brush thinned glue on each side of the snowflake. Sprinkle with glitter, allow to dry and shake off the excess. For the hanger, thread ribbon through a hole at the top and knot the ends together.

Joy Card
(also shown on page 47)

- craft glue
- 5"x6½" white card with envelope
- green and red polka-dot, red Christmas word print and white Christmas word print scrapbook papers
- green jumbo rickrack
- craft knife and cutting mat
- red chalk
- white cardstock
- ¹⁄₁₆" dia. hole punch
- red and white twine
- ¹⁄₈" dia. red brads

1. Cover the card front with red scrapbook paper. Add a polka-dot strip at the bottom and glue rickrack over the paper seam.
2. Cut a 1"x2" opening in the center of a 2"x3" polka-dot paper piece and glue to the center of the card front, 1" from the top. Cut an opening in the card front slightly smaller than the paper opening.
3. Chalk and glue words cut from scrapbook paper to cardstock strips. Punch holes and thread the strips onto twine. Attach the twine to the card front with the brads. Spot glue the strips in place.
4. Cut "JOY" from scrapbook paper. Chalk the edges, glue to a 2"x3" red paper piece and glue to the inside card back, centered in the front opening.

Flocked Candle Box
(also shown on page 54)

- acrylic paint (we used pink)
- paintbrushes
- papier-mâché box with lid (ours is 4½" square)
- tracing and transfer paper
- flocking kit (our kit includes flocking adhesive and assorted colors of flocking fibers)
- fabric glue
- wire-edged ribbon
- wood excelsior
- votive candles

Give this charming box to your favorite candle-lover. Never leave burning candles unattended.

Paint the box and lid. Transfer the pattern (page 147) onto the lid. Working on one small area at a time and following the manufacturer's instructions, flock the pattern. Glue ribbon around the sides of the box and lid and add a bow to the front. Arrange the excelsior and candles in the box.

Gift Wrapping Organizer
(also shown on page 61)

Fig. 1

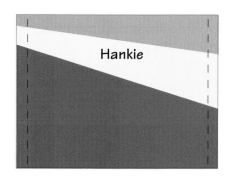

Hankie

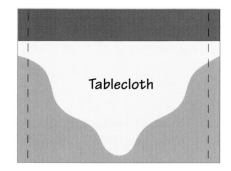

Tablecloth

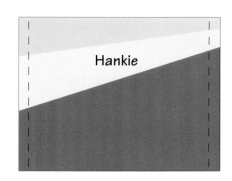

Hankie

Motif A

Motif Scrap Afghan
(also shown on page 55)
*Read Crochet on page 132
before beginning.*

Finished Size: 37³/4" x 61³/4"
(96 cm x 157 cm)

◼◼◻◻ **EASY**

Materials
Medium Weight Yarn
    [3¹/2 ounces, 207 yards
    (100 grams, 188 meters)
    per skein]:
    Taupe - 3 skeins
Scrap colors
    39 ounces, 2,310 yards
    (1,110 grams, 2,113 meters)
    total (we used 7 colors)
Crochet hook, size G (4 mm) **or**
    size needed for gauge
Yarn needle

MEDIUM 4

Gauge: Each Motif = 4³/4"
(12 cm) (from straight edge to
straight edge)

Gauge Swatch: 2¹/2" (6.25 cm)
(from straight edge to straight
edge). Work same as Motif A
through Rnd 2.

Note: Make 113 Motifs total, in
any combination.

Motif A
Rnd 1 (Right side): With first color,
ch 4, 11 dc in fourth ch from hook
(3 skipped chs count as first dc);
join with slip st to first dc, finish
off: 12 dc.

Note: Loop a short piece of yarn
around any stitch to mark Rnd 1
as **right** side.

Rnd 2: With **right** side facing, join
next color with slip st in same st
as joining; ch 3 **(counts as first dc,
now and throughout)**, dc in same
st, 2 dc in next dc, ch 1, (2 dc in
each of next 2 dc, ch 1) around; join
with slip st to first dc, finish off:
24 dc.

To work decrease (uses next 2 dc),
★ YO, insert hook in next dc, YO and
pull up a loop, YO and draw through
2 loops on hook; repeat from ★
once **more**, YO and draw through all
3 loops on hook.

Rnd 3: With **right** side facing, join
next color with slip st in same st
as joining; ch 3, dc in same st,
decrease, 2 dc in next dc, ch 2,
★ 2 dc in next dc, decrease, 2 dc
in next dc, ch 2; repeat from ★
around; join with slip st to first
dc, finish off: 30 sts.

*To work Front Post double treble
crochet (abbreviated FPdtr),* YO
3 times, insert hook from **front** to
back around post of dc indicated
(Fig. 3, page 132), YO and pull up
a loop (5 loops on hook), (YO and
draw through 2 loops on hook)
4 times.

Rnd 4: With **right** side facing, join
next color with slip st in same st as
joining; ch 3, dc in same st and in
next dc, work FPdtr around first dc
on Rnd 1, skip next decrease on
Rnd 3, dc in next dc, 2 dc in next
dc, ch 2, ★ 2 dc in next dc, dc in
next dc, skip next dc on Rnd 1, work
FPdtr around next dc, skip next
decrease on Rnd 3, dc in next dc,
2 dc in next dc, ch 2; repeat from ★
around; join with slip st to first dc,
finish off: 42 sts and 6 ch-2 sps.

Rnd 5: With **right** side facing, join
Taupe with sc in any st (see Joining
with Sc, page 132); sc in next st
and in each st around, working 3 sc
in each ch-2 sp; join with slip st to
first sc, finish off: 60 sc.

(continued on page 118)

Motif B

Motif C

Motif B

With first color, ch 4; join with slip st to form a ring.

To work Beginning Cluster (uses one sp), ch 2, ★ YO, insert hook in sp indicated, YO and pull up a loop, YO and draw through 2 loops on hook; repeat from ★ 2 times **more**, YO and draw through all 4 loops on hook.

To work Cluster (uses one sp), ★ YO, insert hook in sp indicated, YO and pull up a loop, YO and draw through 2 loops on hook; repeat from ★ 3 times **more**, YO and draw through all 5 loops on hook.

Rnd 1 (Right side): Work Beginning Cluster in ring, ch 2, (work Cluster in ring, ch 2) 5 times; join with slip st to top of Beginning Cluster, finish off: 6 ch-2 sps.

Note: Loop a short piece of yarn around any stitch to mark Rnd 1 as **right** side.

Rnd 2: With **right** side facing, join next color with slip st in any ch-2 sp; work (Beginning Cluster, ch 2, Cluster) in same sp, ch 2, (work Cluster, ch 2) twice in each ch-2 sp around; join with slip st to top of Beginning Cluster, finish off: 12 ch-2 sps.

Rnd 3: With **right** side facing, join next color with slip st in last ch-2 sp; work Beginning Cluster in same sp, ch 1, work (Cluster, ch 2, Cluster) in next ch-2 sp, ch 1, ★ work Cluster in next ch-2 sp, ch 1, work (Cluster, ch 2, Cluster) in next ch-2 sp, ch 1; repeat from ★ around; join with slip st to top of Beginning Cluster, finish off: 18 Clusters and 18 sps.

Rnd 4: With **right** side facing, join next color with slip st in any ch-2 sp; ch 1, 3 sc in same sp, sc in next Cluster, (sc in next ch-1 sp, sc in next Cluster) twice, ★ 3 sc in next ch-2 sp, sc in next Cluster, (sc in next ch-1 sp, sc in next Cluster) twice; repeat from ★ around; join with slip st to first sc, finish off: 48 sc.

Rnd 5: With **right** side facing, join Taupe with sc in any sc (see Joining with Sc, page 132); sc in next sc and in each sc around, working 3 sc in center sc of each 3-sc group; join with slip st to first sc, finish off: 60 sc.

Motif C

With first color, ch 5; join with slip st to form a ring.

Rnd 1 (Right side): Ch 1, 12 sc in ring; join with slip st to first sc, finish off.

Note: Loop a short piece of yarn around any st to mark Rnd 1 as **right** side.

To work Beginning Cluster (uses next 2 sc), ch 2, ★ YO, insert hook in next sc, YO and pull up a loop, YO and draw through 2 loops on hook; repeat from ★ once **more**, YO and draw through all 3 loops on hook.

To work Cluster (uses next 2 sc), YO, insert hook in same st, YO and pull up a loop, YO and draw through 2 loops on hook, ★ YO, insert hook in next sc, YO and pull up a loop, YO and draw through 2 loops on hook; repeat from ★ once **more**, YO and draw through all 4 loops on hook.

Rnd 2: With **right** side facing, join yarn with slip st in same st as joining; work Beginning Cluster, ch 4, (work Cluster, ch 4) around, working last leg of last Cluster in same st as Beginning Cluster; join with slip st to top of Beginning Cluster, finish off: 6 Clusters and 6 ch-4 sps.

Rnd 3: With **right** side facing, join next color with slip st in any ch-4 sp; ch 5 **(counts as first dc plus ch 2, now and throughout)**, 3 dc in same sp, ch 1, ★ (3 dc, ch 2, 3 dc) in next ch-4 sp, ch 1; repeat from ★ around, 2 dc in same sp as first dc; join with slip st to first dc, finish off: 36 dc and 12 sps.

Rnd 4: With **right** side facing, join next color with slip st in any ch-2 sp; ch 5, 3 dc in same sp, 3 dc in next ch-1 sp, ★ (3 dc, ch 2, 3 dc) in next ch-2 sp, 3 dc in next ch-1 sp; repeat from ★ around, 2 dc in same sp as first dc; join with slip st to first dc, finish off: 54 dc and 6 ch-2 sps.

Rnd 5: With **right** side facing, join Taupe with sc in any ch-2 sp (see Joining with Sc, page 132); 2 sc in same sp, skip next dc, sc in next 7 dc, ★ 3 sc in next ch-2 sp, skip next dc, sc in next 7 dc; repeat from ★ around; join with slip st to first sc, finish off: 60 sc.

Finishing
Using Placement Diagram as a guide, with Taupe, **wrong** sides together and working through inside loops, whipstitch Motifs together (Fig. 2, page 132), forming 5 vertical strips of 13 Motifs each and 4 vertical strips of 12 Motifs each, beginning in center sc of any corner 3-sc group and ending in center sc of next corner 3-sc group.
Join strips in same manner.

Placement Diagram

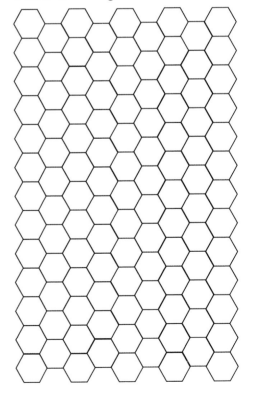

Knitting Tote

(also shown on page 59)
*Read Knit on pages 130-131
before beginning.*

Finished Size: 13" x 21"
(33 cm x 54 cm)

◼◼◼◻ INTERMEDIATE

Materials

Bulky Weight Yarn

[3½ ounces, 142 yards
(100 grams, 129 meters)
per skein]: 3 skeins

Medium Weight Yarn

[6 ounces, 278 yards
(170 grams, 254 meters)
per skein]: 2 skeins

24" (61 cm) Circular knitting
needle, size 10 (6 mm) **or**
size needed for gauge

31" (78.5 cm) Circular knitting
needle, size 10 (6 mm) **or**
size needed for gauge

Two double-pointed knitting
needles, size 10 (6 mm)
for Handles

Markers — six different colors

Yarn needle

Fabric for lining - ⁵/₈ yard (57 cm)

Gauge: In K1, P1 ribbing,
11 sts and 14 rows = 4" (10 cm)

Note: Tote is worked holding one
strand of each yarn held together
and changing length of circular
needle as needed.

Body

With one strand of each yarn held
together and 24" (61 cm) circular
needle, cast on 76 sts; place
marker to mark beginning of rnd
(see Markers and Knitting in the
Round, page 130).

Rnd 1: (K1, P1) around.

Rnd 2: (K1, P1) 6 times, place
different color marker from beginning
marker **(now and throughout)**,
[K1, M1 (Figs. 2a & 2b, page 131), P1]
8 times, place marker, (K1, P1)
11 times, place marker, (K1, M1, P1)
8 times, place marker, (K1, P1)
around: 92 sts.

Rnd 3: (K1, P1) around to next
marker, ★ (K2, P1) around to next
marker, (K1, P1) around to next
marker; repeat from ★ once **more**.

Rnd 4: (K1, P1) around to next
marker, ★ (K1, M1, K1, P1) around to
next marker, (K1, P1) around to next
marker; repeat from ★ once **more**:
108 sts.

Rnd 5: (K1, P1) around to next marker,
★ (K3, P1) around to next marker,
(K1, P1) around to next marker; repeat
from ★ once **more**.

Rnd 6: (K1, P1) around to next
marker, ★ (K1, M1, K2, P1) around to
next marker, (K1, P1) around to next
marker; repeat from ★ once **more**:
124 sts.

Rnd 7: (K1, P1) around to next marker,
★ (K4, P1) around to next marker,
(K1, P1) around to next marker; repeat
from ★ once **more**.

Rnd 8: (K1, P1) around to next
marker, ★ (K1, M1, K3, P1) around to
next marker, (K1, P1) around to next
marker; repeat from ★ once **more**:
140 sts.

Rnd 9: (K1, P1) around to next marker,
★ (K5, P1) around to next marker,
(K1, P1) around to next marker; repeat
from ★ once **more**.

Rnd 10: (K1, P1) around to next
marker, ★ (K1, M1, K3, P1) around to
next marker, (K1, P1) around to next
marker; repeat from ★ once **more**:
156 sts.

Rnd 11: (K1, P1) around to next marker, ★ (K5, P1) around to next marker, (K1, P1) around to next marker; repeat from ★ once **more**.

Repeat Rnd 11 for pattern until Body measures approximately 8" (20.5 cm) from cast on edge.

Top
Rnd 1: (K1, P1) around to next marker, ★ [K1, K2 tog (Fig. 3, page 131), K2, P1] around to next marker, (K1, P1) around to next marker; repeat from ★ once **more**: 140 sts.

Rnd 2: (K1, P1) around to next marker, ★ (K4, P1) around to next marker, (K1, P1) around to next marker; repeat from ★ once **more**.

Rnd 3: (K1, P1) around to next marker, ★ (K1, K2 tog, K1, P1) around to next marker, (K1, P1) around to next marker; repeat from ★ once **more**: 124 sts.

Rnd 4: (K1, P1) around to next marker, ★ (K3, P1) around to next marker, (K1, P1) around to next marker; repeat from ★ once **more**.

Rnd 5: (K1, P1) around to next marker, ★ (K1, K2 tog, P1) around to next marker, (K1, P1) around to next marker; repeat from ★ once **more**: 108 sts.

Rnd 6: (K1, P1) around to next marker, ★ (K2, P1) around to next marker, (K1, P1) around to next marker; repeat from ★ once **more**.

Rnd 7: (K1, P1) around to next marker, ★ (K2 tog, P1) around to next marker, (K1, P1) around to next marker; repeat from ★ once **more**: 92 sts.

Rnd 8: (K1, P1) around to next marker, ★ (K2, P1) around to next marker, (K1, P1) around to next marker; repeat from ★ once **more**.

Rnd 9: (K1, P1) around to next marker, ★ (K2 tog, P1) around to next marker, (K1, P1) around to next marker; repeat from ★ once **more**: 76 sts.

Rnd 10: (K1, P1) around.

Rnd 11: (K1, P1) around to next marker, ★ (K1, P1) 3 times, K2 tog, P2 tog (Fig. 4, page 131), (K1, P1) around to second marker, skipping over first marker; repeat from ★ once **more**: 72 sts.

Rnd 12: (K1, P1) around.

Weave a contrasting color scrap yarn behind knit sts and in front of purl sts on Rnd 11.

Repeat Rnd 12 for 4" (10 cm).

Bind off all sts in pattern.

Handles (make 2)
With one strand of each yarn held together and double-pointed needles, cast on 5 sts.

Row 1: Slide stitches to other end of needle; knit across.

Row 2: Do **not** turn. Slide stitches to other end of needle; knit across.

Repeat Row 2 until Handle measures 26" (66 cm). Bind off all sts.

Finishing
Flatten Body and sew bottom edge. Fold bound off edge 2" (5 cm) to outside and sew in place at marked rnd. Remove contrasting yarn piece. Use yarn to sew Handles to tote. For lining, lay tote flat and use as a pattern to cut two pieces of fabric 1/4" (7 mm) larger than tote on side and bottom edges and 1" (2.5 cm) larger than top edge. Matching right sides and raw edges and using a 1/2" (12 mm) seam allowance, sew pieces together along sides and bottom edge. Clip curved seam allowances. Press 1" (2.5 cm) to wrong side along top edge of Lining. Insert Lining into tote and sew Lining to top edge of tote.

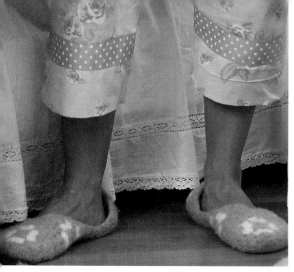

Mommy & Me PJ's with Tote Bags

(also shown on page 60)

- Mom's and child's straight-leg sweatpants
- kraft paper
- flannel
- ribbon or rickrack for trim (optional)
- 3/4"w elastic
- large safety pin
- polyester batting
- liquid fray preventative
- ribbon and rope for tote bag drawstrings

Pair these PJ pants with a comfy T-shirt. Match right sides and use a 1/2" seam allowance unless otherwise indicated.

Pants

1. For each pair of pants, match the outside leg edges and fold the sweatpants in half (Fig. 1). For a pattern, stretch the waistband of the pants and draw around the pants on kraft paper. Add 1 1/2" at the top, 3/4" on each side and desired amount at the bottom for the hem. (We added 1" for the boy's and 3" for the girl's and trimmed the legs of Mom's PJ's for cropped pants with a 3" hem.) Cut out the pattern.
2. Use the pattern to cut 4 flannel pieces (2 of these in reverse).

Fig. 1   **Fig. 2**

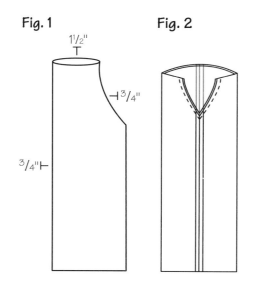

3. Sew the pieces together in pairs along the outer side edges. Turn and sew the hem, adding trim as desired. Sew each inseam.
4. Turn one leg right side out and slip it inside the other, aligning the seams at the center (Fig. 2). Sew the crotch seam and pull the inside leg out; do not turn right side out.
5. Fold the top edge of the pants 1/4", then 1 1/4" to the wrong side and sew along the folded edge, leaving an opening for inserting elastic. Cut the elastic 1" larger than the person's waist. Use the safety pin to thread elastic through the waistband; overlap and sew the ends together. Sew the opening closed and turn right side out.

Tote Bags

1. For each bag, cut a 20"x40" flannel rectangle. Cut two 12" diameter circles from flannel and one from batting.
2. Sew trim 3" from one long edge of the rectangle. Sew the short edges of the rectangle together to form a tube. Fold the top edge 4" to the wrong side and sew along the raw edge. Sew around the tube 1" above the stitching to make the casing (Fig. 1). Cut a small opening in the casing in the bag front for a drawstring to go through and apply fray preventative to the opening.

Fig. 1

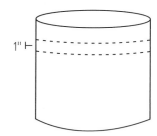

3. With the flannel circles right side out, sandwich and sew the batting circle between the flannel circles. Pleating the tube at the seam to fit, pin, then sew the circles to the bottom of the bag. Remove the pins and turn right side out.
4. Use the safety pin to thread the ribbon or rope drawstring through the casing.

Granny Square Slippers

(also shown on page 60)
Read Crochet on page 132 before beginning.

Finished Size:

Small   9" (23 cm)
Medium   9¹/₂" (24 cm)
Large   10" (25.5 cm)

▰▰▱▱ **EASY**

Materials

Medium Weight Yarn
  [3¹/₂ ounces, 223 yards
  (100 grams, 205 meters)
  per skein]: 1 skein each color
Crochet hook as indicated below
  or size needed for gauge
  Size Small and Medium: size F
  (3.75 mm)
  Size Large: size H (5 mm)
Yarn needle
Small, medium or large flip-flops

Gauge: Size Small, Square =
  3¹/₂" (9 cm)
Size Medium, Square = 3³/₄" (9.5 cm)
Size Large, Square = 4¹/₂" (11.5 cm)

Gauge Swatch: Work same as Square.

Note: Slippers are made with 6 Squares per slipper. Our photography models were made by using 5 Square A and 1 Square B (toe) for size Small and 6 Square C for sizes Medium and Large. However, any combination of the Squares can be used to make the slippers.

SQUARE A (ONE COLOR)

With desired color, ch 3, join with slip st to form a ring.

Rnd 1 (Right side): Ch 3 **(counts as first dc, now and throughout)**, 2 dc in ring, (ch 1, 3 dc in ring) 3 times, sc in first dc to form last ch-1 sp: 12 dc and 4 ch-1 sps.

Note: Loop a short piece of yarn around any stitch to mark Rnd 1 as **right** side.

Rnd 2: Ch 3, 2 dc in last ch-1 sp made, (3 dc, ch 1, 3 dc) in next 3 ch-1 sps, 3 dc in same sp as first dc, sc in first dc to form last ch-1 sp: 24 dc and 4 ch-1 sps.

Rnd 3: Ch 3, 2 dc in last ch-1 sp made, skip next 3 dc, 3 dc in sp **before** next dc (Fig. 1, page 132), ★ (3 dc, ch 1, 3 dc) in next ch-1 sp, skip next 3 dc, 3 dc in sp **before** next dc; repeat from ★ 2 times **more**, 3 dc in same sp as first dc, sc in first dc to form last ch-1 sp; do **not** finish off: 36 dc and 4 ch-1 sps.

Size Small Only

Rnd 4: Ch 1, 3 sc in last ch-1 sp made, sc in next 9 dc, (3 sc in next ch-1 sp, sc in next 9 dc) 3 times; join with slip st to first sc, finish off: 48 sc.

Size Medium Only

Rnd 4: Ch 2 **(counts as first hdc)**, 2 hdc in last ch-1 sp made, hdc in next 9 dc, (3 hdc in next ch-1 sp, hdc in next 9 dc) 3 times; join with slip st to first hdc, finish off: 48 hdc.

Size Large Only

Rnd 4: Ch 3, 2 dc in last ch-1 sp made, (skip next 3 dc, 3 dc in sp **before** next dc) twice, ★ (3 dc, ch 1, 3 dc) in next ch-1 sp, (skip next 3 dc, 3 dc in sp **before** next dc) twice; repeat from ★ 2 times **more**, 3 dc in same sp as first dc, ch 1; join with slip st to first dc, finish off: 48 dc and 4 ch-1 sps.

(continued on page 124)

SQUARE B (TWO COLORS)

With first color, ch 3; join with slip st to form a ring.

Rnd 1 (Right side): Ch 3 **(counts as first dc, now and throughout)**, 2 dc in ring, ch 1, (3 dc in ring, ch 1) 3 times; join with slip st to first dc, finish off: 12 dc and 4 ch-1 sps.

Note: Loop a short piece of yarn around any stitch to mark Rnd 1 as **right** side.

Rnd 2: With **right** side facing, join next color with dc in any ch-1 sp (see *Joining with Dc, page 132*); (2 dc, ch 1, 3 dc) in same sp, (3 dc, ch 1, 3 dc) in next 3 ch-1 sps, sc in first dc to form last ch-1 sp; do **not** finish off: 24 dc and 4 ch-1 sps.

Rnd 3: Ch 3, 2 dc in last ch-1 sp made, skip next 3 dc, 3 dc in sp *before* next dc (*Fig. 1, page 132*), ★ (3 dc, ch 1, 3 dc) in next ch-1 sp, skip next 3 dc, 3 dc in sp *before* next dc; repeat from ★ 2 times **more**, 3 dc in same sp as first dc, sc in first dc to form last ch-1 sp; do **not** finish off: 36 dc and 4 ch-1 sps.

Size Small Only

Rnd 4: Ch 1, 3 sc in last ch-1 sp made, (sc in next 9 dc, 3 sc in next ch-1 sp) 3 times, sc in last 9 dc; join with slip st to first sc, finish off: 48 sc.

Size Medium Only

Rnd 4: Ch 2 **(counts as first hdc)**, 2 hdc in last ch-1 sp made, (hdc in next 9 dc, 3 hdc in next ch-1 sp) 3 times, hdc in last 9 dc; join with slip st to first hdc, finish off: 48 hdc.

Size Large Only

Rnd 4: Ch 3, 2 dc in last ch-1 sp made, (skip next 3 dc, 3 dc in sp *before* next dc) twice, ★ (3 dc, ch 1, 3 dc) in next ch-1 sp, (skip next 3 dc, 3 dc in sp *before* next dc) twice; repeat from ★ 2 times **more**, 3 dc in same sp as first dc, ch 1; join with slip st to first dc, finish off: 48 dc and 4 ch-1 sps.

SQUARE C (THREE COLORS)

With first color, ch 3; join with slip st to form a ring.

Rnd 1 (Right side): Ch 3 **(counts as first dc, now and throughout)**, 2 dc in ring, ch 1, (3 dc in ring, ch 1) 3 times; join with slip st to first dc, finish off: 12 dc and 4 ch-1 sps.

Note: Loop a short piece of yarn around any stitch to mark Rnd 1 as **right** side.

Rnd 2: With **right** side facing, join next color with dc in any ch-1 sp (see *Joining with Dc, page 132*); (2 dc, ch 1, 3 dc) in same sp, (3 dc, ch 1, 3 dc) in next 3 ch-1 sps; join with slip st to first dc, finish off: 24 dc and 4 ch-1 sps.

Rnd 3: With **right** side facing, join next color with dc in any ch-1 sp; 2 dc in same sp, skip next 3 dc, 3 dc in sp *before* next dc (*Fig. 1, page 132*), ★ (3 dc, ch 1, 3 dc) in next ch-1 sp, skip next 3 dc, 3 dc in sp *before* next dc; repeat from ★ 2 times **more**, 3 dc in same sp as first dc, sc in first dc to form last ch-1 sp, do **not** finish off: 36 dc and 4 ch-1 sps.

Size Small Only
Rnd 4: Ch 1, 3 sc in last ch-1 sp made, sc in next 9 dc, (3 sc in next ch-1 sp, sc in next 9 dc) 3 times; join with slip st to first sc, finish off: 48 sc.

Size Medium Only
Rnd 4: Ch 2 (**counts as first hdc**), 2 hdc in same sp, hdc in next 9 dc, (3 hdc in next ch-1 sp, hdc in next 9 dc) 3 times; join with slip st to first hdc, finish off: 48 hdc.

Size Large Only
Rnd 4: Ch 3, 2 dc in last ch-1 sp made, (skip next 3 dc, 3 dc in sp **before** next dc) twice, ★ (3 dc, ch 1, 3 dc) in next ch-1 sp, (skip next 3 dc, 3 dc in sp **before** next dc) twice; repeat from ★ 2 times **more**, 3 dc in same sp as first dc, ch 1; join with slip st to first dc, finish off: 48 dc and 4 ch-1 sps.

Assembly
With coordinating color, **wrong** sides together, and working through inside loops only, whipstitch Squares together (Fig. 2, page 132) forming 2 vertical strips of 2 Squares each; then whipstitch strips together. Form heel by joining Square 5 to corner (Diagram 1); then form toe by joining Square 6 to opposite corner and to Square 1 and Square 3 (Diagram 2).

Diagram 1 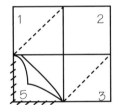 **Diagram 2**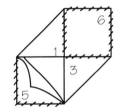

Possible color variations on Square C				
Size	Rnd 1	Rnd 2	Rnd 3	Rnd 4
For Medium	Dk Pink	White	Petal Pink	Petal Pink
For Large	Lt Blue	White	Lt Blue	Lt Blue

Felting
1. Set your top-loading washing machine for a HOT wash and COLD rinse cycle. Add about a tablespoon of laundry detergent.

2. With the flip-flops inside the slippers, place them in a tight-mesh lingerie or sweater bag (a pillowcase tied at the top works too!) and toss into the machine. Check the slippers every 2-3 minutes during the wash cycle to keep an eye on the amount of felting and the final size. A properly felted item has shrunk to the desired size and the stitches are no longer easy to see. You may want to wear rubber gloves for this, as the water can be pretty hot.

3. Once the slippers have felted to your satisfaction, spin out the wash water and then run the slippers through the cold rinse part of the cycle. Most people do not let their projects go through the spin portion of the cycle as this can set permanent creases.

4. Now that the slippers are felted, they need to be shaped. While wet, stretch the slippers to the finished size. Let the slippers air dry which may take a day or two depending on the weather.

Apple Bags

(also shown on page 65)
- red print fabric
- $1/4$"w green ribbon
- plastic zipping bags filled with Cranberry Cider Mix (page 64)
- tracing paper
- green textured cardstock
- black fine-point permanent pen
- craft glue
- cinnamon sticks

Match right sides and use a $1/2$" seam allowance unless otherwise indicated.

1. For each bag, cut a $6^1/2$"x12" fabric piece. For the casing, sew the short edges $3/4$" to the wrong side. Matching short edges, fold the fabric in half. Stopping at the casings, sew the sides together.

2. To form the bottom corners, match the side seams to the bottom fold. Sew across each corner $1^1/2$" from the point (Fig. 1).

Fig. 1

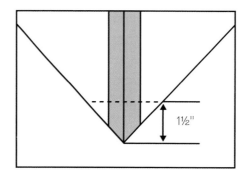

$1^1/2$"

3. Knot the ends of a 22" ribbon length and thread the ribbon through the casing. Turn the bag right side out.
4. Place the mix in the bag. Pull the ribbon ends to gather the bag closed and tie into a bow.
5. Use the pattern on page 144 and cut cardstock leaves. Write a message on a leaf and glue the leaves to a cinnamon stick. Insert the stick in the bag opening.

Oatmeal Cookie Box

(also shown on page 68)
- empty oatmeal box with lid (ours measures 4" dia.x$7^1/8$"h)
- craft glue
- green plaid and red print scrapbook paper
- white vellum
- deckle-edged scissors
- green textured cardstock
- square brads
- $1^1/2$"w sheer white ribbon
- tracing paper
- dark green and yellow cardstock scraps
- 3 yellow E-beads
- black fine-point permanent pen
- $1/8$" dia. hole punch
- "To:" and "From:" stamps
- black ink pad
- Jo Ann's Walnut-Oatmeal Cookie Mix in a sealed cellophane bag (page 68)

1. Cover the box and lid inset with plaid paper.
2. For the label, use a computer to print the title on vellum and cut to $2^1/4$"x$4^1/4$" with the deckle-edged scissors. Attach the corners of the vellum to a 3"x5" deckle-edged green cardstock piece with brads.

Glue the label to the box. Threading the ribbon between the label layers and gluing the ends at the back, wrap the ribbon around the box.

3. Use the patterns on page 145 and cut two large red paper flowers and one green cardstock leaf set for the box and a small red paper flower and green cardstock leaf set for the lid. Bending the petal ends up slightly and gluing at the centers only, layer and glue the large flower pieces to the box. Glue thin dark green cardstock strips and the beads to the flower center. Set aside the small flower pieces.

4. Matching short edges, fold a 3³/₄" x7" green cardstock piece in half and cut out a round card to fit the lid. Write the mix instructions inside. Glue the small flower and leaves and yellow cardstock circles to a plaid paper circle and stamp a message. Glue the circle to the card front and the card to the lid. Place the mix in the box.

Truffle Box
(also shown on page 69)
- double-sided tape
- Christmas scrapbook papers and sticker
- 2"x8" white jewelry gift box
- rub-on letters
- Chocolate-Raspberry Truffles (page 69)
- foil candy cups
- ³/₈"w ribbons
- textured cardstock
- ¹/₈" dia. hole punch
- twine

Tape scrapbook paper to the lid and the inside bottom of the box. Add a message on the lid with rub-ons and the sticker. Place truffles in candy cups inside the box. Replace the lid and knot ribbons around the box. Make a cardstock name tag and add rub-ons. Punch a hole in the tag and tie it onto the ribbons with twine.

Holly Tag
(also shown on page 69)

For the tag, scalloping the edge of the large circle, cut 2³/₄", 2³/₈" and 2¹/₄" diameter scrapbook paper circles. Layer and glue the circles together. Cut holly leaves from scrapbook paper (pattern on page 145). Spell "for you" on the leaves with rub-on letters. Adhere the leaves and ¹/₂" diameter scrapbook paper "berries" on the tag with glue and foam dots. Attach an eyelet to the tag. Stack Chocolate-Wrapped Peppermint Cookies (page 69) in a cellophane bag and tie the tag onto the bag with velvet ribbon.

General Instructions

Embroidery Stitches

Blanket Stitch:
Referring to Fig. 1, bring the needle up at 1. Keeping the thread below the point of the needle, go down at 2 and come up at 3. Continue working as shown in Fig. 2.

Chain Stitch:
Referring to Fig. 3, bring the needle up at 1; take the needle down again at 1 to form a loop. Bring the needle up at 2; take the needle down again at 2 to form a second loop. Bring the needle up at 3 and repeat as in Fig. 4. Anchor the last chain with a small straight stitch.

French Knot:
Referring to Fig. 5, bring the needle up at 1. Wrap the floss once around the needle and insert the needle at 2, holding the floss end with non-stitching fingers. Tighten the knot; then, pull the needle through the fabric, holding the floss until it must be released. For a larger knot, use more strands; wrap only once.

Lazy Daisy Stitch:
Bring the needle up at 1; take the needle down again at 1 to form a loop and bring the needle up at 2. Keeping the loop below the point of the needle (Fig. 6), take the needle down at 3 to anchor the loop.

Fig. 1

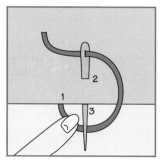

Fig. 2

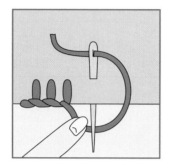

Fig. 3

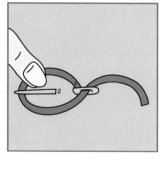

Fig. 4

Fig. 5

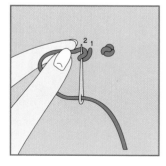

Fig. 6

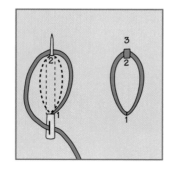

Fig. 7

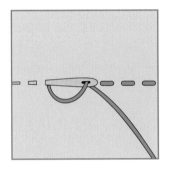

Fig. 8

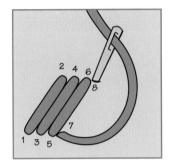

Running Stitch:

Referring to Fig. 7, make a series of straight stitches with the stitch length equal to the space between stitches.

Satin Stitch:

Referring to Fig. 8, come up at odd numbers and go down at even numbers with the stitches touching but not overlapping.

Fig. 9

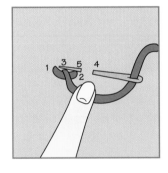

Fig. 10

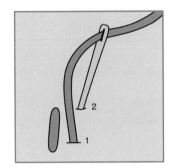

Stem Stitch:

Referring to Fig. 9, come up at 1. Keeping the thread below the stitching line, go down at 2 and come up at 3. Go down at 4 and come up at 5.

Straight Stitch:

Referring to Fig. 10, come up at 1 and go down at 2.

Fig. 11

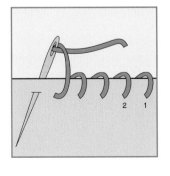

Whipstitch:

Bring the needle up at 1; take the thread around the edge of the fabric and bring the needle up at 2. Continue stitching along the edge of the fabric (Fig. 11).

Knit

Abbreviations

cm	centimeters	P	purl
K	knit	Rnd(s)	Round(s)
M1	make one	st(s)	stitch(es)
mm	millimeters	tog	together

★ — work instructions following ★ as many **more** times as indicated in addition to the first time.

( ) or [ ] — work enclosed instructions **as many** times as specified by the number immediately following **or** work all enclosed instructions in the stitch or space indicated **or** contains explanatory remarks.

colon (:) — the number(s) given after a colon at the end of a row or round denote(s) the number of stitches you should have on that row or round.

Gauge

Exact gauge is essential for proper size. Before beginning your project, make the sample swatch given in the individual instructions in the yarn and needle specified. After completing the swatch, measure it, counting your stitches and rows or rounds carefully. If your swatch is larger or smaller than specified, make another, changing needle size to get the correct gauge. Keep trying until you find the size needles that will give you the specified gauge.

Markers

As a convenience to you, we have used markers to help distinguish the beginning of a pattern or round. Place markers as instructed. You may use purchased markers or tie a length of contrasting color yarn around the needle. When you reach a marker on each round, slip it from the left needle to the right needle; remove it when no longer needed.

Fig. 1

Knitting in the Round

Using a circular needle, cast on all stitches as instructed. Untwist and straighten the stitches on the needle before beginning the first round. Place a marker after the last stitch to mark the beginning of a round. Hold the needle so the skein of yarn is attached to the stitch closest to the right hand point. To begin working in the round, knit the stitches on the left hand point (Fig. 1).

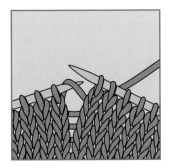

Fig. 2a

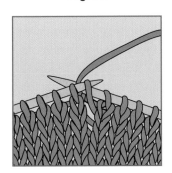

Fig. 2b

Make One

(abbreviated M1)

Insert the left needle under the horizontal strand between the stitches from the front (Fig. 2a). Then knit into the back of the strand (Fig. 2b).

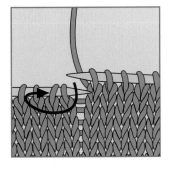

Fig. 3

Fig. 4

Knit 2 Together

(abbreviated K2 tog)

Insert the right needle into the **front** of the first two stitches on the left needle as if to **knit** (Fig. 3); then, **knit** them together as if they were one stitch.

Purl 2 Together

(abbreviated P2 tog)

Insert the right needle into the **front** of the first two stitches on the left needle as if to **purl** (Fig. 4); then, **purl** them together as if they were one stitch.

Crochet

Abbreviations

ch(s)	chain(s)	Rnd(s)	Round(s)
cm	centimeters	sc	single crochet(s)
dc	double crochet(s)	sp(s)	space(s)
hdc	half double crochet(s)	st(s)	stitch(es)
mm	millimeters	YO	yarn over

★ — work instructions following ★ as many **more** times as indicated in addition to the first time.

( ) — work all enclosed instructions in the stitch or space indicated **or** contains explanatory remarks.

colon (:) — the number(s) given after a colon at the end of a row or round denote(s) the number of stitches you should have on that row or round.

Fig. 1

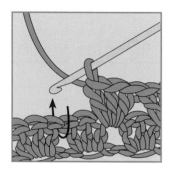

Fig. 2

Fig. 3

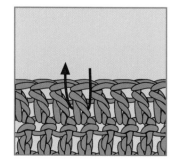

Gauge

Exact gauge is essential for proper size or fit. Before beginning your project, make the sample swatch given in the individual instructions in the yarn and hook specified. After completing the swatch, measure it, counting your stitches and rows or rounds carefully. If your swatch is larger or smaller than specified, make another, changing hook size to get the correct gauge. Keep trying until you find the size hook that will give you the specified gauge.

Joining with Sc

When instructed to join with sc, begin with a slip knot on the hook. Insert the hook in the stitch or space indicated, YO and pull up a loop, YO and draw through both loops on the hook.

Joining with Dc

When instructed to join with dc, begin with a slip knot on the hook. YO, holding loop on hook, insert hook in loop or space indicated, YO and pull up a loop (3 loops on hook), (YO and draw through 2 loops on hook) twice.

Working in Space Before a Stitch

When instructed to work in a space before a stitch, insert hook in space indicated by arrow (Fig. 1).

Whipstitch

With **wrong** sides together, sew through both pieces once to secure the beginning of the seam, leaving an ample yarn end to weave in later. Insert the needle from **right** to **left** through one strand on each piece (Fig. 2). Bring the needle around and insert it from **right** to **left** through the next strand on both pieces. Repeat along the edge, being careful to match stitches and rows.

Front Post

Work around post of stitch indicated, inserting hook in direction of arrow (Fig. 3).

Making Patterns

When the entire pattern is shown, place tracing paper over the pattern and draw over the lines. For a more durable pattern, use a permanent marker to draw over the pattern on stencil plastic.

When only half of the pattern is shown (indicated by a solid blue line on the pattern), fold the tracing paper in half. Place the fold along the solid blue line and trace the pattern half. Turn the folded paper over and draw over the traced lines on the remaining side. Unfold the pattern and cut it out.

Fig. 1

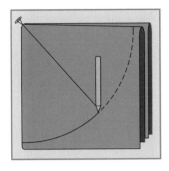

Making a Fabric Circle

Matching right sides, fold the fabric square in half from top to bottom and again from left to right. Tie one end of a length of string to a fabric marking pen; insert a thumbtack through the string at the length indicated in the project instructions. Insert the thumbtack through the folded corner of the fabric. Holding the tack in place and keeping the string taut, mark the cutting line (Fig. 1).

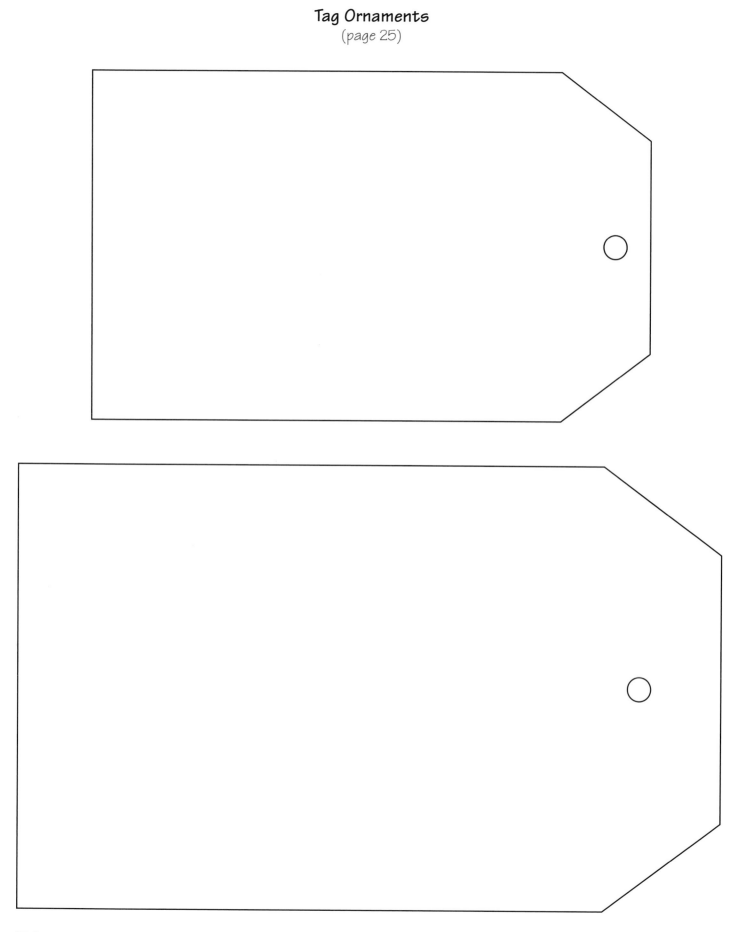

Polka-Dot Stocking
(page 27)

135

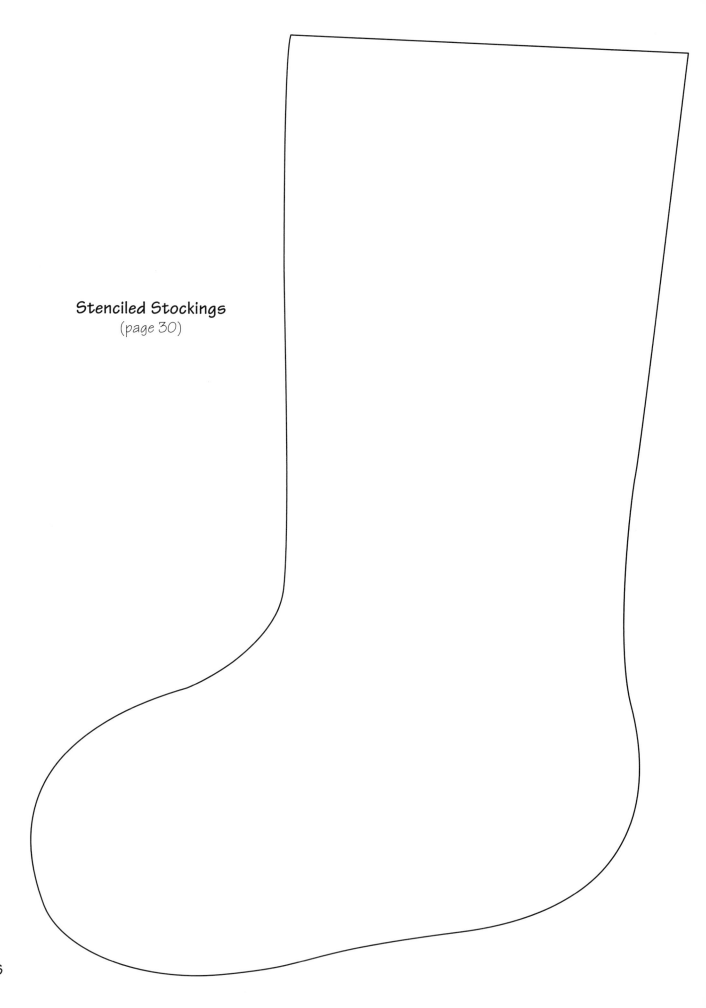

Stenciled Stockings
(page 30)

136

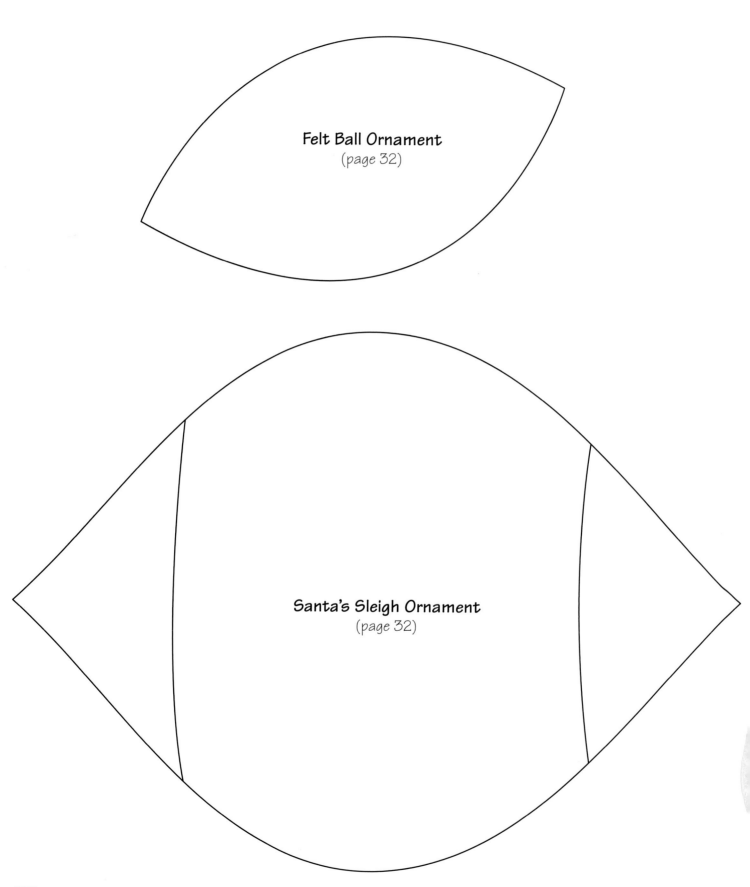

Felt Ball Ornament
(page 32)

Santa's Sleigh Ornament
(page 32)

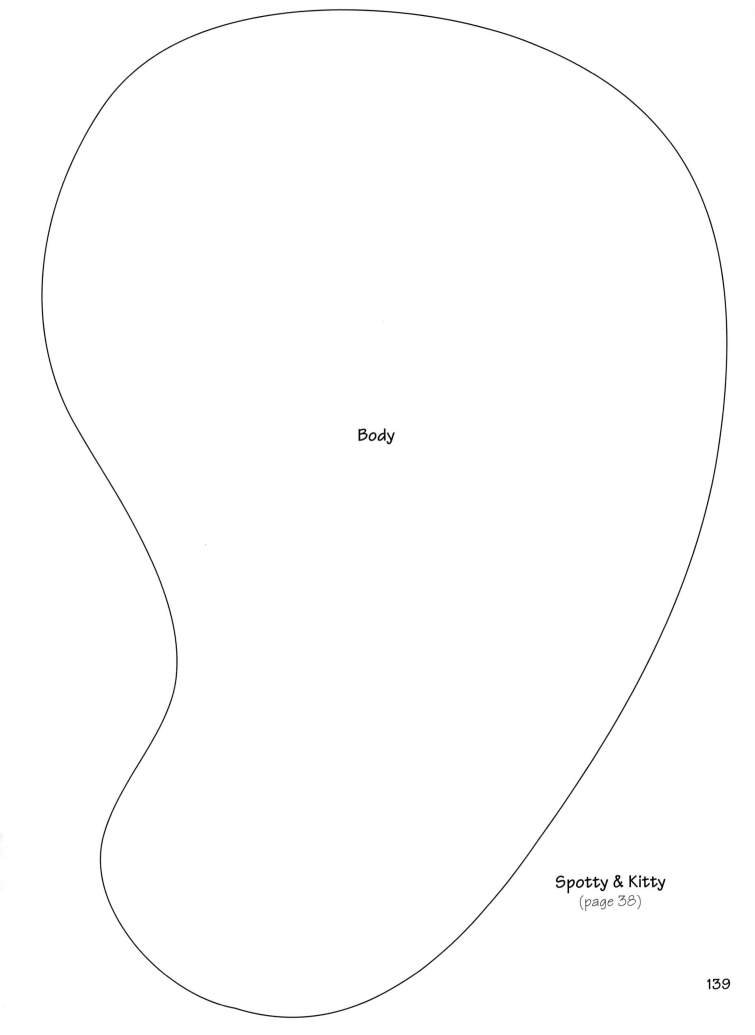

Body

Spotty & Kitty
(page 38)

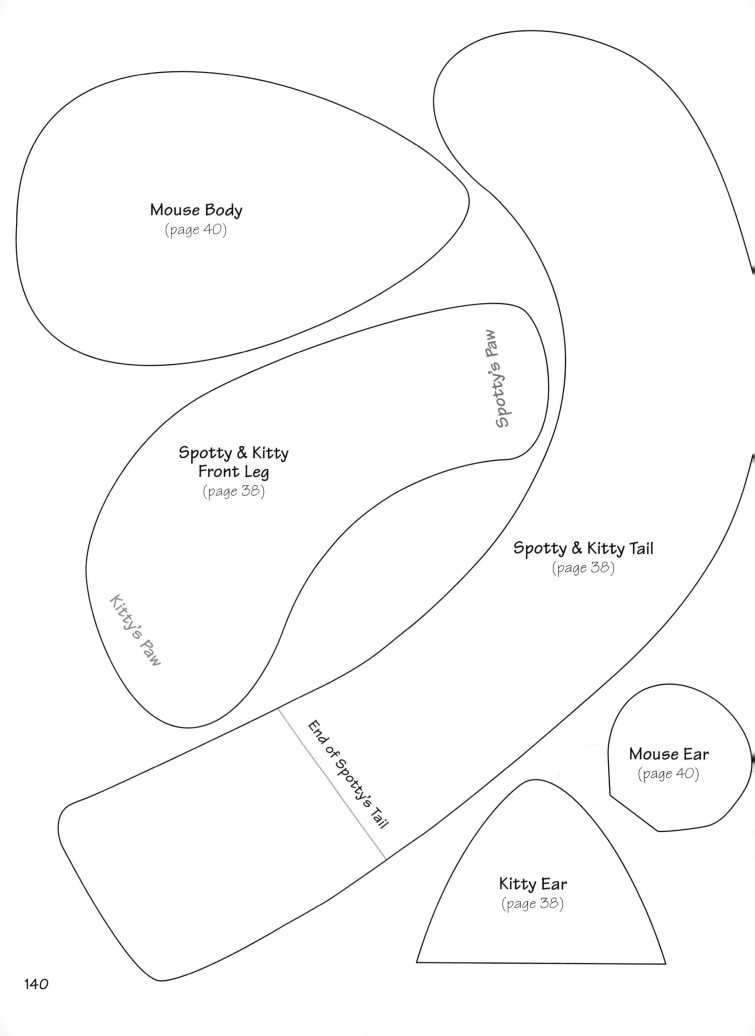

Mouse Body
(page 40)

Spotty & Kitty
Front Leg
(page 38)

Spotty's Paw

Kitty's Paw

Spotty & Kitty Tail
(page 38)

End of Spotty's Tail

Mouse Ear
(page 40)

Kitty Ear
(page 38)

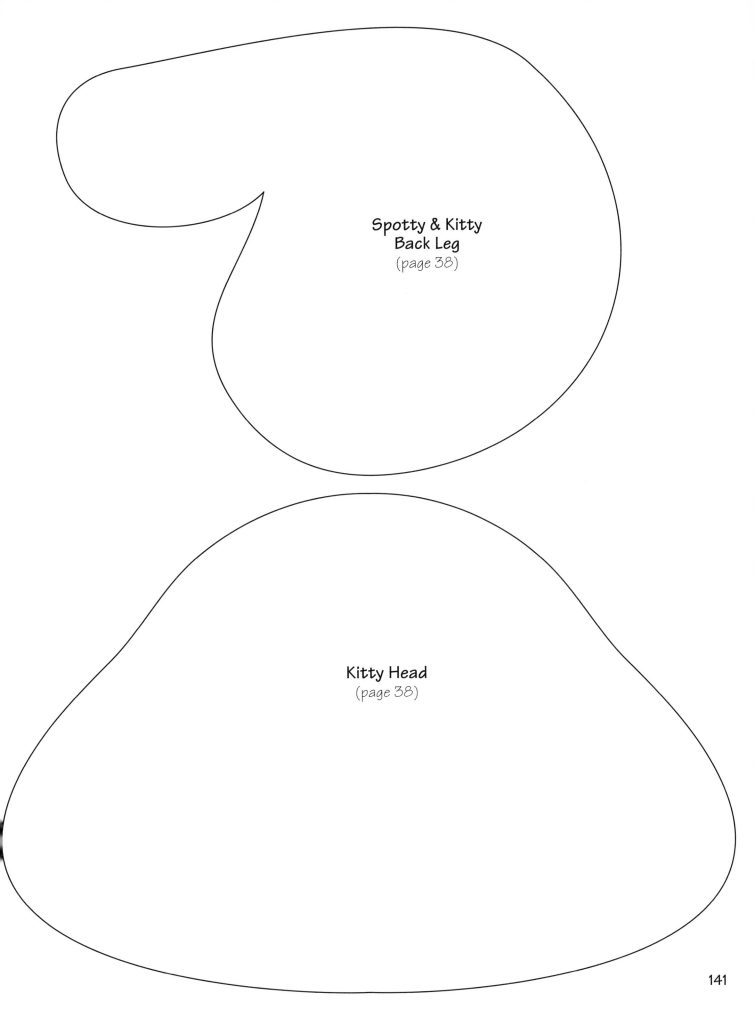

Spotty & Kitty
Back Leg
(page 38)

Kitty Head
(page 38)

141

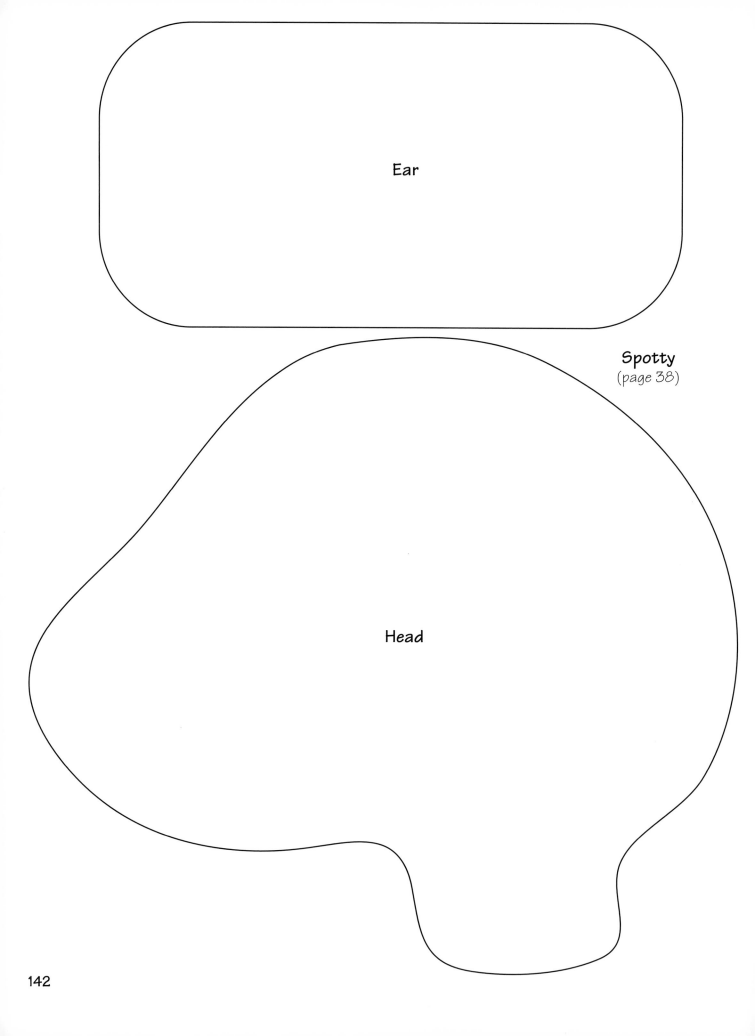

Ear

Head

Spotty
(page 38)

142

Kitty I.D. Tag Ornaments
(page 41)

Pet Silhouette Ornaments
(page 40)

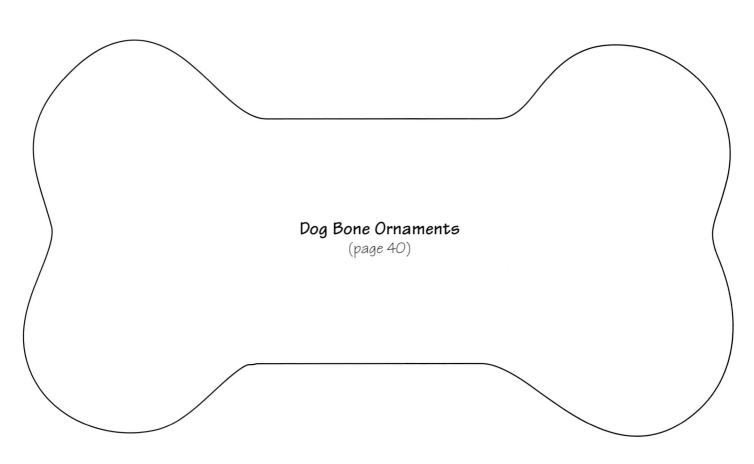

Dog Bone Ornaments
(page 40)

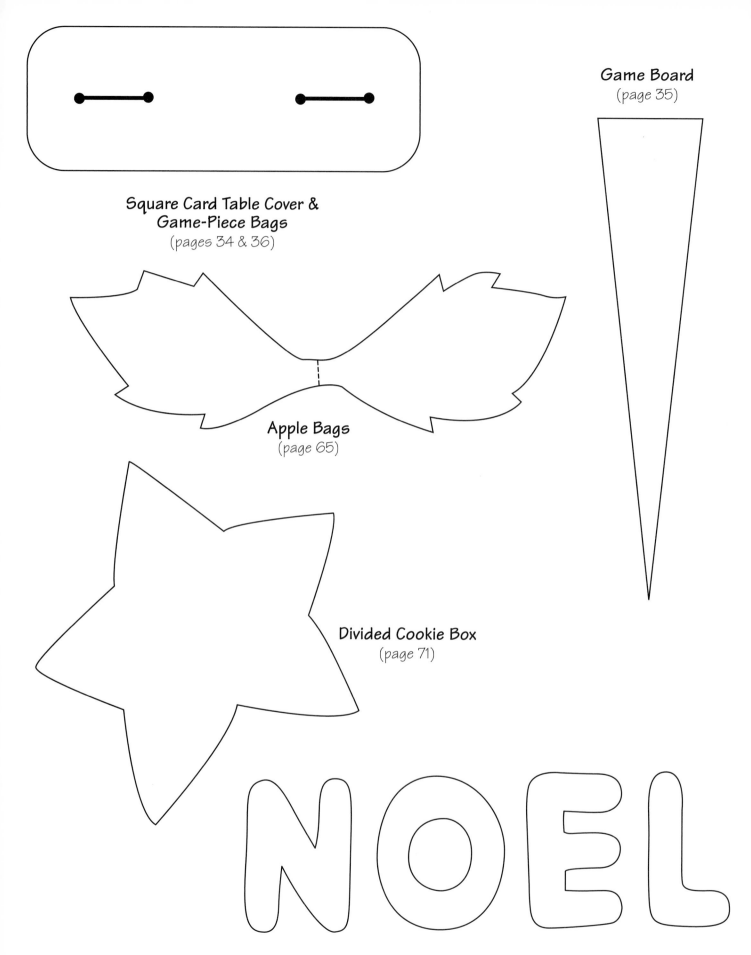

Game Board
(page 35)

**Square Card Table Cover &
Game-Piece Bags**
(pages 34 & 36)

Apple Bags
(page 65)

Divided Cookie Box
(page 71)

NOEL

144

Chocolate-Peanut Butter Cookies
(page 71)

Cellophane Bag Topper
(page 75)

Honey Jars
(page 74)

Holly Tag
(page 69)

Chinese Take-Out Box
(page 66)

Oatmeal Cookie Box
(page 68)

Small Leaves

Large Leaves

Large Flower

Small Flower

Appliquéd Bag
(page 63)

Top

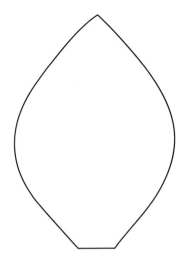

Egg Cup Pin Cushion
(page 58)

Flocked Candle Box
(page 54)

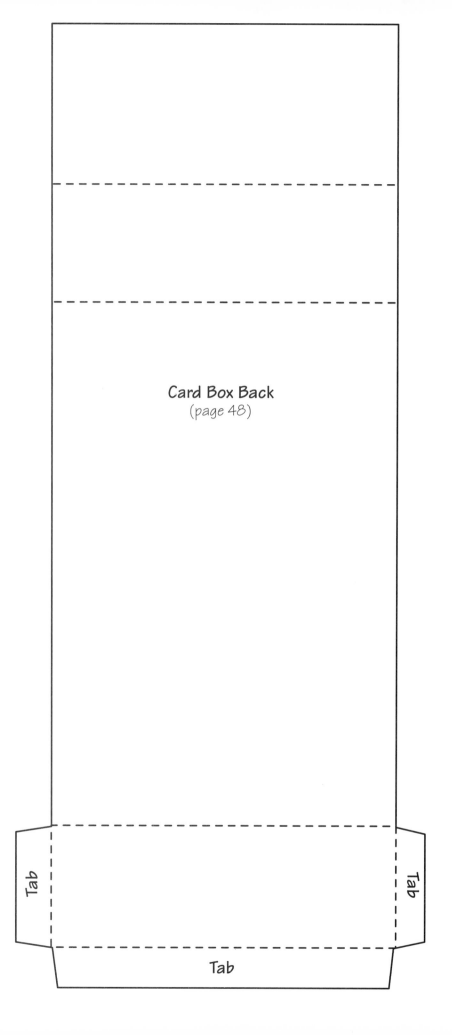

Card Box Back
(page 48)

Tab

Tab

Tab

Tab

Card Box Front
(page 48)

Tab

XOXO Package
Embellishment
(page 43)

Snowflake Ornament
(page 42)

Jingle Bell Postcard
(page 49)

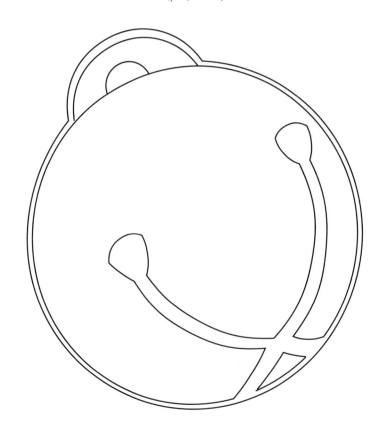

Velvet Jewelry Pouch
(page 62)

Stitching Diagram

— Ecru Stem Stitch

⟋ Red Lazy Daisy

— Green Stem Stitch

⟋ Green Lazy Daisy

Flower Brooch
(page 58)

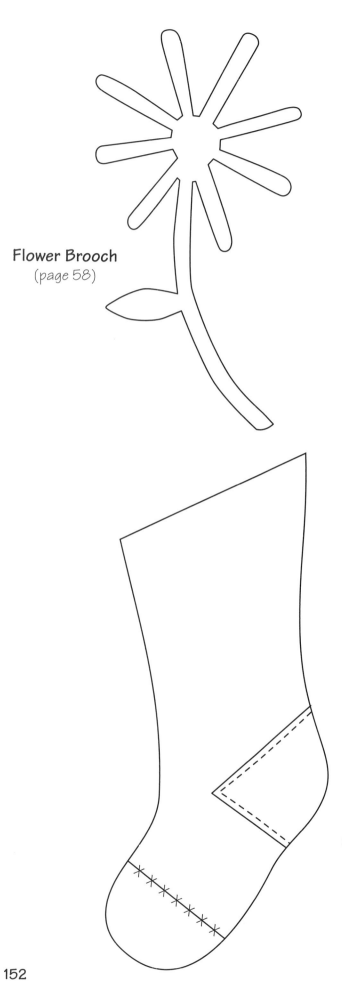

No Peeking Tag
(page 44)

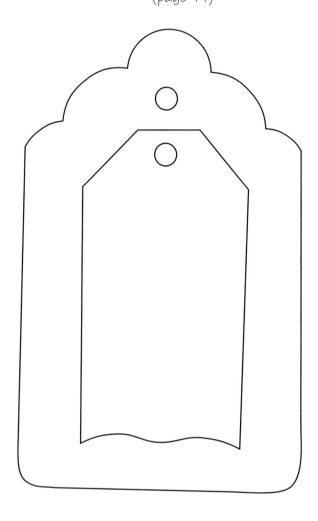

Stocking Stuffer Money Holder
(page 46)

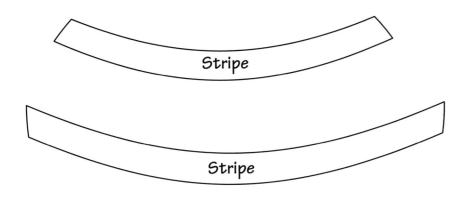

Stripe

Stripe

Ornament Gift Card Holder
(page 45)

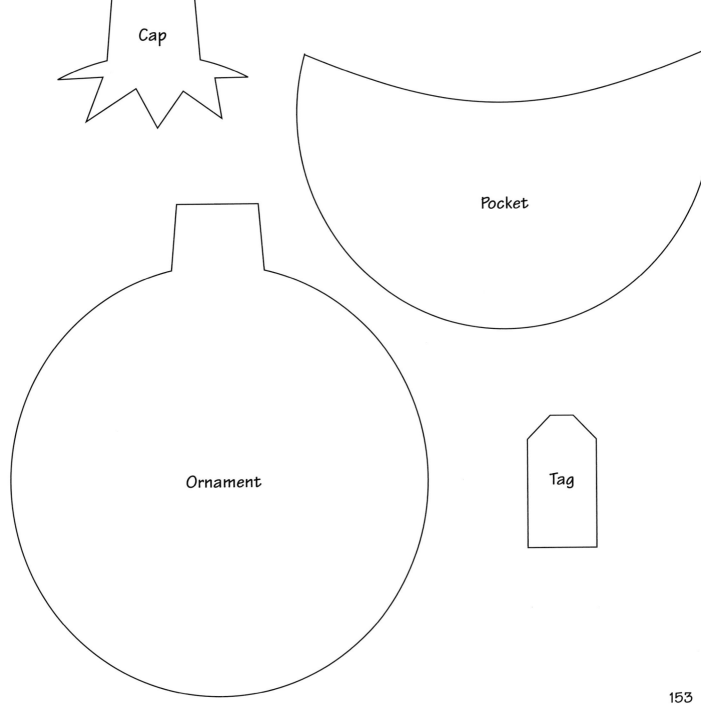

Cap

Pocket

Ornament

Tag

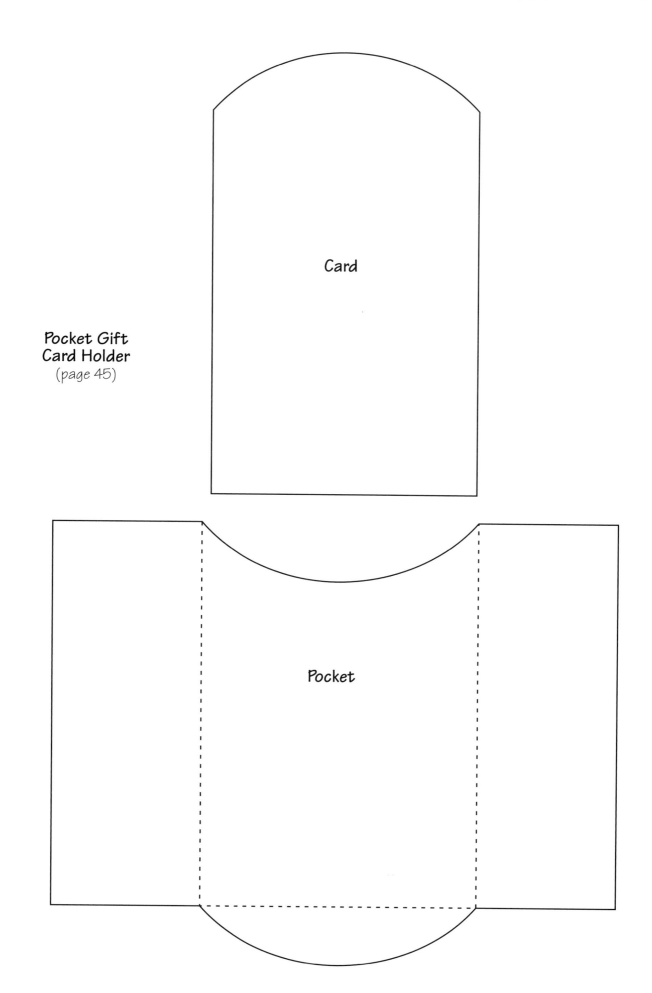

Card

Pocket Gift
Card Holder
(page 45)

Pocket

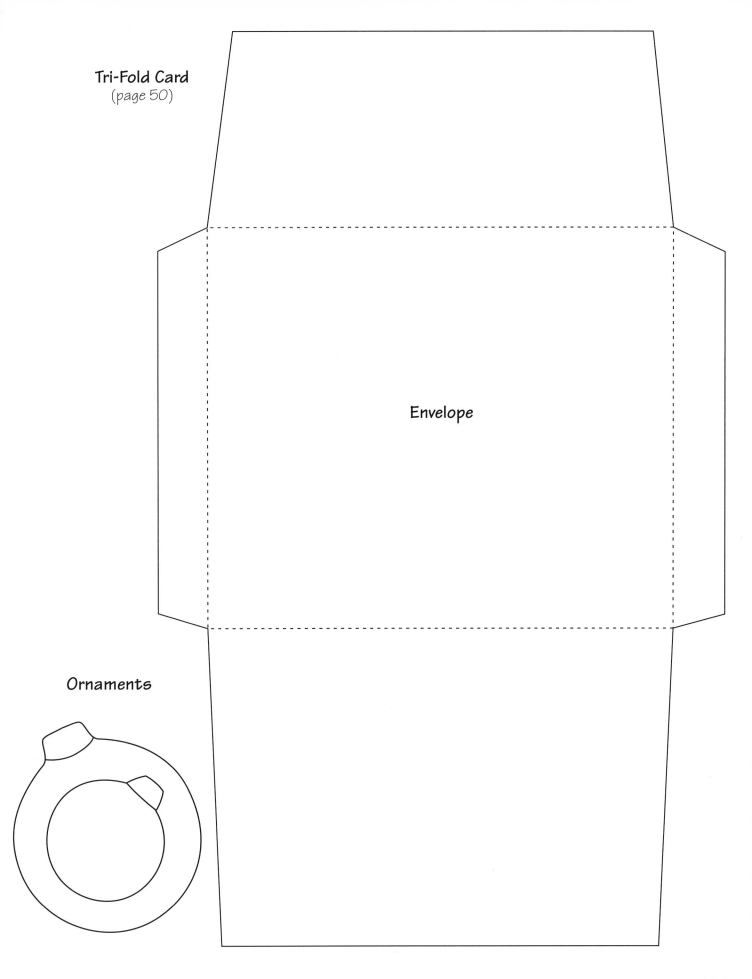

Tri-Fold Card
(page 50)

Envelope

Ornaments

Project Index

On the Front Cover
Rest a candleholder in the top of a ribbon-wrapped jar filled with sugary gumdrops. Tie on a scrapbook paper tag for gifting.

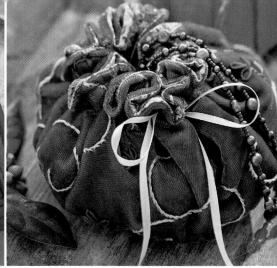

Recipe Index

Credits

We want to extend a warm thank you to the people who allowed us to photograph some of our projects at their homes: Bill & Nancy Appleton, Duncan & Nancy Porter, Elizabeth Rice and Anne & Randy Stocks.

We want to especially thank photographers Jerry R. Davis of Jerry Davis Photography, Jason Masters, Mark Mathews Photography and Ken West Photography, all of Little Rock, Arkansas, for their excellent work.

We would like to recognize the following companies for providing some of the materials and tools we used to make our projects: Raggedy Junction for Meltie Feltie's hand-dyed wool felt; DonJer for flocking adhesive and fibers; Dan River, Inc. for flannel; Saral® Paper Corp. for transfer paper; and Lion Brand® Yarn Company and Patons Yarn for yarn.

Special thanks go to Marianna Crowder for crocheting the Motif Scrap Afghan and Janet Akins & Sue Galucki for crocheting the Granny Square Slippers.

We extend a special word of thanks to Kay Meadors for designing the Knitting Tote and Knit 'N' Purl Shop of Edina, MN, for designing the Granny Square Slippers.

If these cozy Christmas ideas have inspired you to look for more Gooseberry Patch® publications, treat yourself to a Gooseberry Patch product catalog, which is filled with cookbooks, candles, enamelware, bowls, gourmet goodies and hundreds of other country collectibles. For a subscription to "A Country Store in Your Mailbox©," visit www.gooseberrypatch.com.